T0316735

Cambridge Elements

Elements in Gender and Politics
edited by
Tiffany D. Barnes
University of Texas at Austin
Diana Z. O'Brien
Washington University in St. Louis

THE POLITICS OF BATHROOM ACCESS AND EXCLUSION IN THE UNITED STATES

Sara Chatfield
University of Denver

CAMBRIDGE
UNIVERSITY PRESS

Shaftesbury Road, Cambridge CB2 8EA, United Kingdom

One Liberty Plaza, 20th Floor, New York, NY 10006, USA

477 Williamstown Road, Port Melbourne, VIC 3207, Australia

314–321, 3rd Floor, Plot 3, Splendor Forum, Jasola District Centre, New Delhi – 110025, India

103 Penang Road, #05–06/07, Visioncrest Commercial, Singapore 238467

Cambridge University Press is part of Cambridge University Press & Assessment, a department of the University of Cambridge.

We share the University's mission to contribute to society through the pursuit of education, learning and research at the highest international levels of excellence.

www.cambridge.org
Information on this title: www.cambridge.org/9781009539562

DOI: 10.1017/9781009429085

First published 2024

A catalogue record for this publication is available from the British Library.

ISBN 978-1-009-53956-2 Hardback
ISBN 978-1-009-42906-1 Paperback
ISSN 2753-8117 (online)
ISSN 2753-8109 (print)

The Politics of Bathroom Access and Exclusion in the United States

Elements in Gender and Politics

DOI: 10.1017/9781009429085
First published online: December 2024

Sara Chatfield
University of Denver

Author for correspondence: Sara Chatfield, sara.chatfield@du.edu

Abstract: The past twenty years have seen an explosion of state laws focused on bathroom access, including laws that both restrict and expand the ability of people to access basic needs in public. Through an analysis of several distinct state-level policies that regulate bathrooms along the dimensions of gender and gender roles, gender identity, and disability, the author argues that bathroom access is an important aspect of citizenship, signaling both physical and symbolic exclusion and inclusion. Social citizenship requires that individuals and groups be able to fully take part in the public sphere, yet denying toilet access means that individuals can only exist in public for as long as they can "hold it." Thus, ensuring equal access to bathrooms – or denying it to targeted groups – becomes a powerful way for society to define who is a full citizen and to indicate who belongs and who doesn't in public spaces.

This Element also has a video abstract: www.cambridge.org/chatfield_abstract

Keywords: state politics, gender, gender identity, disability, bathrooms

ISBNs: 9781009539562 (HB), 9781009429061 (PB), 9781009429085 (OC)
ISSNs: 2753-8117 (online), 2753-8109 (print)

Contents

1 Introduction

Lauren Barrow's son, Cameron, was diagnosed with a brain tumor at ten months old. As a result, he developed multiple disabilities – throughout his life, he used a wheelchair to get around and wore a diaper. But, as he grew older, Barrow found that baby changing tables were no longer adequate or safe. She, along with other moms of disabled kids, worked together as part of the Colorado Accessibility Project to advocate for the installation of larger, universal changing stations. Barrow wrote about bathroom access: "If a person is unable to use a toilet, they can go out to places, but only for a little while … A safe, clean, dignified place to use the restroom, or get a diaper changed, means these people can go out and experience the world."[1] And, although Colorado doesn't yet require universal changing stations, five other states have passed legislation that does.

Meanwhile, states around the country have introduced and enacted so-called "bathroom bills" that target trans people – especially trans youth – just for using the bathroom. These laws restrict access to bathrooms in certain locations, particularly schools, based on sex assigned at birth. For Julien Noble and his family, Iowa's bathroom bill was the final straw in their decision to move out-of-state. While Julien could have stayed in Iowa and travelled to receive gender affirming health care after his state banned it, being forced to use the girls' restroom on a daily basis at school was not feasible.[2] And Julien's story is not unique: more broadly, trans students who were denied access to the bathroom matching their gender identity at school reported both physical and mental health consequences, including dehydration and urinary tract infections, due to trying to avoid eating and drinking during the school day.[3]

Both of these examples are part of a larger trend. The past twenty years have seen an explosion of state laws focused on bathrooms access in the United States, including laws that both restrict and expand the ability of people to access basic needs in public. These laws include anti-trans bathroom bills, expanded availability of gender neutral bathrooms, requirements for both baby and adult changing tables, provisions for free menstrual products in restrooms, and greater access for individuals

---

[1] Lauren Barrow, correspondence with author, June 16, 2023.

[2] T. Gabriel, "Two families got fed up with their states' politics: So they moved out," *New York Times*, October 7, 2023, www.nytimes.com/2023/10/07/us/politics/politics-states-moving.html.

[3] M. M. Lewis and S. E. Eckes, "Storytelling, leadership, and the law: Using amicus briefs to understand the impact of school district policies and practices related to transgender student inclusion," *Educational Administration Quarterly* 56, no. 1 (2020): 65.

with inflammatory bowel disease and related disabilities, among others. Bathrooms as a site of political and legal struggle are not a new phenomenon, but that struggle has expanded into a variety of novel policy areas in recent years.

Discrimination in access to bathroom facilities has long been a political issue in the United States. Without access to appropriate restrooms, people are limited in how long they can leave private homes and how far they can travel. They are unable to fully access educational and employment opportunities and their political and social engagement are curtailed. And, those access rights are debated and decided largely in state and local contexts – they are the result of political decisions and they vary across the country depending on partisanship, lobbying efforts, and other group dynamics. When bathroom access issues intersect with identity, entire groups may be excluded from activities central to daily life.

In this Element, I argue that bathroom access is a key component of social citizenship and analyze variation across US state legislative politics. In the first section, I review bathroom access politics in American political development, addressing the ways in which identity has been used to police public bathroom access from the Jim Crow era forward. Then, I analyze contemporary bathroom policies as they relate to gender and gender roles, gender identity, and disability accessibility.[4] Finally, I conclude with considering how social citizenship can help us draw connections in bathroom access policies across issue areas, including in a global context and in more explicitly class-based policy areas.

1.1 Bathrooms and Social Citizenship

Access to adequate bathrooms when in public, educational, and employment spaces is crucial for individuals to enjoy full social citizenship. Social citizenship goes beyond formal or legal citizenship and requires that individuals not only be legal members of society but also have full access to opportunities and dignity. Importantly, because bathroom policies vary dramatically from state to state and city to city, individuals may experience different levels of inclusion on the dimension of social citizenship even when they enjoy equal national citizenship in a formal sense.

---

[4] As I use the terms here, gender refers to "the characteristics of women, men, girls and boys that are socially constructed … [including] norms, [behaviors] and roles associated with being a woman, man, girl or boy." Relatedly but distinct, "[g]ender identity refers to a person's deeply felt, internal and individual experience of gender, which may or may not correspond to the person's physiology or designated sex at birth." See World Health Organization, "Gender and Health." accessed March 19, 2024, www.who.int/health-topics/gender (2024).

Social citizenship as an idea was first developed by T. H. Marshall in his 1950 essay on citizenship and social class in Britain.[5] Marshall differentiated between three components of full citizenship: civil, political, and social. Civil citizenship includes individual rights such as free speech and property rights. Political citizenship encompasses the ability to participate fully in democratic politics. Finally, Marshall described social citizenship as "the whole range from the right to a modicum of economic welfare and security to the right to share to the full in the social heritage and to live the life of a civilized being according to the standards prevailing in the society."[6] In his original essay, Marshall focused primarily on economic class and social safety net policies such as housing, education, welfare, and wages.

Since 1950, the term social citizenship (along with closely related concepts such as social inclusion and exclusion) has been leveraged primarily in European contexts, and the specific application of these terms differs across countries.[7] Although scholars sometimes emphasize that social citizenship encompasses a wider definition of citizenship than solely class-related concerns such as income equality and the alleviation of poverty, many articles focus primarily on government policies that relate to class and welfare.[8] For example, Hilary Silver and S. M. Miller write that social exclusion may be unrelated to poverty, but also emphasize primarily policies and indicators related to economic provision when discussing the alleviation of social exclusion.[9]

Still, the concepts of social exclusion and social citizenship have the potential to extend beyond exclusively class- and economic-based considerations. Koen Vleminckx and Jos Berghman, for example, emphasize that social exclusion results in "the isolation of individuals and groups from the mainstream of opportunities society has to offer" and argue that government policy can reduce social exclusion by "removing various kinds of active and passive boundaries that obstruct the participation of

---

[5] T. H. Marshall and T. Bottomore, *Citizenship and social class* (London: Pluto Press, 1992).

[6] Marshall and Bottomore, *Citizenship and social class*, 16.

[7] H. Silver and S. M. Miller, "Social exclusion: The European approach to social disadvantage," *Indicators* 2, no. 2 (2003): 5–21; K. Vleminckx and J. Berghman, "Social exclusion and the welfare state: An overview of conceptual issues and policy implications," in *Social exclusion and European policy*, ed. D. Mayes, J. Berghman, and R. Salais (Northampton: Elgar, 2001), 27–46; D. Béland, "The social exclusion discourse: Ideas and policy change," *Policy & Politics* 35, no. 1 (2007): 123–139.

[8] See, for example, I. Bloemraad, W. Kymlicka, M. Lamont, and L. S. S. Hing "Membership without social citizenship? Deservingness & redistribution as grounds for equality," *Daedalus* 148, no. 3 (2019): 73–104; P. Dwyer, *Understanding social citizenship: Themes and perspectives for policy and practice* (Bristol: The Policy Press, 2004).

[9] Silver and Miller, "Social exclusion."

individuals in the economic, social, and political life of the society."[10] Jane Millar similarly writes that at the core of social exclusion is the "inability of people to participate in the society in which they live."[11] Some scholars and activists have centered social citizenship on the concept of dignity.[12] This broader idea of social citizenship and exclusion from it clearly can stem from both class-based and non-class-based causes. Living a life of dignity and sharing fully in society's opportunities means more than not being impoverished, and individuals can be excluded along a number of dimensions, including but not limited to their class status.

In particular, criticism of the social citizenship literature has included the concern that this work is overly focused on a normative male, able-bodied citizen. Because Marshall's discussion of social citizenship focuses on class inequality as the primary axis on which exclusion from full social citizenship may occur, it ignores other structural factors such as gender, race, and disability.[13] Indeed, in the US context, social citizenship for white men was defined in part through their domination over and even ownership of other human beings.[14]

By expanding the lens and considering multiple dimensions along which individuals may be denied social citizenship, we can consider a wider array of policies that may either advance or restrict social citizenship. Social citizenship requires that individuals be able to fully take part in public life. As such, access to the physical spaces where citizenship takes place impacts the extent to which both individuals and groups are able to become wholly integrated in society. In particular, equal access to safe bathrooms outside the home has clear implications for social citizenship.

Some scholarship on bathrooms analyzes connections to social citizenship and related concepts. Judith Plaskow discusses "the ways in which access to toilets is a prerequisite for full public participation and citizenship."[15] Tanya Lovell Banks argues that the availability of public toilets is inextricably linked to dignity and equality.[16] Relatedly, Alexander Davis's research on gender and toilets explores the ways in which the presence or absence of bathrooms sends signals to groups about inclusion, exclusion, and collective

---

[10] Vleminckx and Berghman, "Social exclusion," 46.

[11] J. Millar, "Social exclusion and social policy research: Defining exclusion," in *Multidisciplinary handbook of social exclusion research*, ed. D. Abrams, J. Christian, and D. Gordon (New York: John Wiley & Sons, 2008), 3.

[12] R. Lister, "Inclusive citizenship: Realizing the potential," *Citizenship Studies* 11, no. 1 (2007): 53.

[13] N. Fraser and L. Gordon, "Contract versus charity: Why is there no social citizenship in the United States?" *Socialist Review* 22, no. 3 (1993): 45–67. Lister, "Inclusive citizenship," 53.

[14] Fraser and Gordon, "Contract versus charity," 56.

[15] J. Plaskow, "Embodiment, elimination, and the role of toilets in struggles for social justice," *CrossCurrents* 58, no. 1 (2008): 53.

[16] T. L. Banks, "The disappearing public toilet," *Seton Hall Law Review* 50, no. 4 (2019): 1061–1094.

societal values.[17] Each of these works emphasizes that people cannot be full members of society without equal access to bathrooms in public spaces and other spaces outside the home.[18] And, although each emphasizes different identities and forms of exclusion, we can start to see how all of these seemingly disparate distributions of bathroom access impact the same aspect of citizenship by linking exclusion to biological needs.

Without access to restroom facilities outside the home, individuals are limited in their ability to participate fully in public life, including missing out on employment and education opportunities, the ability to travel, and even simply socializing in public for longer than they can "hold it." As Simon Bryant writes, "To deny someone access to a public bathroom is to make that person disappear, to erase their public presence."[19] And, of course, access to toilets outside the home – historically and in contemporary society – is not randomly distributed. In the US context, Plaskow writes that "the absence of toilet facilities has signaled to blacks, to women, to workers, to people with disabilities, to transgender people, and to homeless people that they are outsiders to the body politic and that there is no room for them in public space."[20]

The power to make decisions about who to include or exclude is also not randomly distributed. In the contemporary United States, partisan polarization is sometimes but not always an important factor for understanding the passage and implementation of bathroom-access policies. I find that policies most clearly intersecting with "culture wars" issues related to gender identity, as well as policies that impact K-12 children in school, are more likely to be enacted by legislative votes divided along partisan lines. This is unsurprising given the recent rise in attacks on the trans community by the Republican party, as well as the broader politicization of educational institutions around issues such as book banning and the teaching of "divisive topics." Thus, partisan polarization on bathroom-access policies can be seen as part of these broader trends.

Some other types of bathroom-related policies tend to enjoy more bipartisan support. Yet, this does not mean there is universal access along these dimensions – here, lobbying efforts and the willingness of legislative entrepreneurs to

---

[17] A. K. Davis, *Bathroom battlegrounds: How public restrooms shape the gender order* (Oakland: University of California Press, 2020).

[18] On this point see also B. P. Bagagli, T. V. Chaves, and M. G. Zoppi Fontana, "Trans women and public restrooms: The legal discourse and its violence," *Frontiers in Sociology* 6 (2021): 1–14; R. M. Weinmeyer, "Lavatories of democracy: Recognizing a right to public toilets through international human rights and state constitutional law," *University of Pennsylvania Journal of Constitutional Law* 26, no. 2 (2024): 402–470.

[19] B. Simon, "The trouble with bathrooms," *Modern American History* 4, no. 2 (2021): 205.

[20] Plaskow, "Embodiment," 61.

pursue less politically salient measures create an uneven policy landscape across the nation. Interestingly, some bathroom policies are being incorporated into model building and plumbing codes, which has the potential to depoliticize the policy adoption process even further in the future.

My understanding of social citizenship as it relates to bathrooms has two interrelated components. First is the physical denial of access to public spaces for longer than one can "hold it." Annabel Cooper and coauthors call this the "leash" of the bladder.[21] If an acceptable bathroom is not available in public, people have the choices to remain at home, to try to avoid drinking liquids (with related consequences for their physical health), to risk public urination or defecation – which is illegal in many cities and can lead to sex offender registration – or, as Barrow puts it, to go out, "but only for a little while." Ultimately, none of these choices are good ones and lead to the physical exclusion of many from the public sphere. The second aspect of social citizenship is the more psychological and symbolic injury to dignity, inclusion, and belonging that stems from a lack of toilet access, especially when it is targeted at specific groups. Although both components may not always be present in every piece of bathroom-related legislation, they are often connected in practice.

In one recent example, a young Black child was arrested, taken to a local jail, and sentenced to probation for urinating behind his mother's car when no public restroom was available.[22] This incident involved the physical removal of the child from public by police, who locked him in a jail cell for about an hour. And, of course, beyond the immediate injustice are the lasting impacts on the child of trauma, contact with the criminal justice system, and mistrust of police, all of which are connected to dignity and a feeling of full belonging in society.[23] Throughout this Element, I will highlight how both the physical and symbolic aspects of social citizenship are impacted by bathroom access legislation.

1.2 Data and Methods

This Element focuses on legislative enactments in US state legislatures through the conclusion of each state's 2023 legislative session. I analyze contemporary

---

[21] A. Cooper, R. Law, J. Malthus, and P. Wood, "Rooms of their own: Public toilets and gendered citizens in a New Zealand city, 1860–1940," *Gender, Place and Culture: A Journal of Feminist Geography* 7, no. 4 (2000): 426.

[22] A. Planas, "Race played role in sentencing of black child, 10, for urinating in public, lawyer says," *NBC News*, December 13, 2023, www.nbcnews.com/news/nbcblk/race-played-role-sen tencing-black-child-10-urinating-public-lawyer-say-rcna129631.

[23] M. Bedigan, "Ten-year-old boy gets harsh sentence for public urination," *The Independent*, December 14, 2023, www.the-independent.com/news/world/americas/crime/boy-sentence-pub lic-urination-b2464417.html; J. Gordon, "A 10-year-old in Mississippi who was arrested for urinating in public gets probation and a book report assignment," *CNN*, December 13, 2023, www.cnn.com/2023/12/13/us/mississippi-boy-arrested-urinating-book-report/index.html.

policies in three broad areas: gender and gender roles, gender identity, and disability. Within each broad area, I identified specific policies in which state legislatures engaged in significant activity from the 1990s through the 2020s. Each state policy identified either expands or restricts access to bathrooms along some dimension, and there is no federal mandate so that adoption is uneven across states. Then, for each policy, I identified the first date in which each state enacted that policy. Statute dates were determined using a combination of interest group bill tracking resources, state legislative websites, state statute books, and news sources.

For the first relevant policy enacted in each state, I collected the full statute text, which allows me to describe the specific content of state policies and patterns across states. I also collected data on each final passage vote or decision. These were primarily roll call votes, although some statutes passed through unanimous consent, voice votes, or similar procedures. This data allows me to determine whether final passage votes on various bathroom access-related policies tended to be bipartisan or polarized on the basis of partisanship. I calculated the percentage of final chamber decisions on each policy that were unanimous and the percentage that were party unity votes (meaning that the majority of one party voted in favor of the law, and the majority of the other party voted against it).

In addition to this quantitative data, I surveyed interest group websites and news sources to provide additional qualitative context. Although the focus here is on state legislative activity, I also discuss national policies as well as judicial and bureaucratic venues as necessary to understand the broader political environment in which policies were enacted. The goal of this multi-method approach is first a descriptive one: to (1) describe the content of bathroom access-related legislation and variations across states and (2) identify the geographic and temporal spread of each policy. In addition to understanding the basic contours of bathroom access policies in the states, I then go on to analyze the role of interest groups and partisanship in the policy process and to explain how ideas central to social citizenship shaped the policy debate.

The policy areas addressed in this Element are actively being debated in state legislatures around the nation. State legislators continue to introduce bills and governors continue to sign new policies into law. For the purposes of this manuscript, I consider bathroom access-related legislation that was signed into law during 2023 state legislative sessions or earlier. Of course, the debate and passage of these laws will not stop in 2024. Data on state-level policies for each issue area addressed in this Element is available on Harvard Dataverse and will be periodically updated with newly passed state-level legislation: https://doi.org/10.7910/DVN/KV7ERA. Details about data collection can be found in the Data Appendix.

2 Bathrooms in American Political Development

Social citizenship in the United States has long been connected to struggles over access to public accommodations, including bathrooms. Public accommodations are generally defined under the law as places that – though they may be privately owned – are open to and serve the public. This includes businesses such as hotels, restaurants, movie theaters, and sports stadiums.[24] While civil rights laws protect equal access to public accommodations, the Fourteenth Amendment protects equal access to state owned and controlled spaces.[25] The broader struggle over access to public spaces and who gets to control that access is illustrated by the contention over equal and adequate access to bathrooms throughout US history.

This section provides a historical overview of bathrooms in US politics. It begins with a discussion of racial segregation of bathrooms in both the Jim Crow South as well as in Northern cities. During this same period, sex-segregated bathrooms also began to be legislated upon for the first time. The section concludes with a discussion of the history of public restroom provision, beginning in the Progressive Era. Each of these topics is connected and linked to one another, and together they tell a story about struggles for inclusion and access to public spaces that spans from the 1880s through the present.

As will be evident from this account, arguments about bathroom access implicate both public health and sanitation, as well as moral framings around inclusion, equity, and dignity (or their opposites). As Alexander Davis argues, cleanliness, morality, and democracy have long been intertwined in United States history. In the mid nineteenth century, "[p]ublicly showcasing signals of one's moral stature subsequently came to function as a way for individuals to convey their commitment to themselves and their country in simultaneity, allowing regular bathing and 'clean' toileting practices to proliferate in popularity."[26] Over time, efforts to increase sanitation and "cleanliness" among immigrant and Black communities continued to meld public health and moralizing rhetoric, and became a mechanism for these groups to prove their belonging as Americans.[27] Both the historical examples in this section and the analysis of contemporary bathroom laws that follows reveal that both framings remain highly relevant for understanding how bathrooms are employed by the politically powerful to regulate citizenship.

---

[24] Civil Rights Act of 1964, Public Law 88–352, 78 Stat. 241.

[25] See, among many examples, *McLaurin v. Oklahoma State Regents*, 339 U.S. 637 (1950).

[26] Davis, *Bathroom battlegrounds*, 31.

[27] S. Hoy, *Chasing dirt: The American pursuit of cleanliness* (New York: Oxford University Press, 1997), 87–122.

2.1 Racial Segregation of Bathroom Facilities

When we think about segregated bathrooms and the exclusion of specific groups from bathrooms in US history, racially segregated bathrooms during the Jim Crow era often come to mind first. Ranging from 1881 through 1964, twenty-six states throughout the US – including but not limited to the South – legally required separation of white and Black Americans in many spaces.[28] Jim Crow laws as well as social custom enforced racial segregation in a huge variety of public spaces, including bathrooms. Of course, Jim Crow was not only about bathrooms; they were only one small part of "an entire legal system dedicated to making African Americans second-class citizens."[29]

Bathrooms specifically became a flashpoint in multiple political struggles, including the desegregation of workplaces during World War II and the desegregation of schools after *Brown v. Board of Education*, 347 US 483 (1954). In 1943, white workers at a Baltimore electric plant struck over being forced to share a bathroom with a Black colleague. During the strike, white male employees claimed that segregated bathrooms were needed to "protect endangered white women."[30] White women, for their part, argued that "sharing toilets meant the mixing of bodily fluids and the pollution of purer white bodies by over-sexed Black bodies," putting them at risk of venereal disease.[31] As a result of the war-time strike, federal troops had to take over operation of the factory for months, and ultimately the plant re-segregated its bathrooms in the face of ongoing resistance from white workers.[32] Resistance to integrated facilities by white workers was not limited to the South. The year after the Baltimore strike, white Detroit rubber workers struck over similar issues, demanding that Black women machinists be forced to use segregated toilets.[33] White workers in Ohio and California similarly "refused to share toilets with Black workers" when their companies integrated.[34]

Integrated bathrooms and locker rooms also became a significant talking point among white supremacists opposed to the integration of schools, including Little Rock's Central High in 1957. School officials and local segregationist groups argued that racially integrated bathrooms – enforced by federal officials – would expose white girls to venereal disease and even sexual assault.[35] Phoebe

---

[28] L. V. Tischauser, *Jim Crow laws* (Santa Barbara: Greenwood, 2012), xi.

[29] Tischauser, *Jim Crow*, 168.   [30] Simon, "The trouble with bathrooms," 203.

[31] Simon, "The trouble with bathrooms," 204.

[32] E. Yellin, *Our mothers' war: American women at home and at the front during World War II* (New York: Free Press, 2004), 201–202.

[33] E. Boris, "'You wouldn't want one of 'em dancing with your wife': Racialized bodies on the job in World War II," *American Quarterly* 50, no. 1 (1998): 94.

[34] Simon, "The trouble with bathrooms," 202.

[35] P. Godfrey, "Bayonets, brainwashing, and bathrooms: The discourse of race, gender, and sexuality in the desegregation of Little Rock's Central High," *The Arkansas Historical*

Godfrey writes that this rhetoric among white communities was part of a larger moral panic around contamination and contagion, with vulnerable white girls portrayed as being in danger not only of physical illness but sexual corruption from both Black girls and federal troops.[36]

The use of rhetoric related to contamination and disease also appears in the legal record. For example, in October of 1960, the city of Memphis agreed to mostly integrate its libraries in response to a combination of petitions, sit-ins, protests, and legal action.[37] But, the libraries continued to segregate their bathrooms, arguing that segregating city-owned bathrooms was a valid exercise of the police power in the interest of public health, to protect white patrons from venereal diseases that they – theoretically – might catch from Black patrons. A federal court ultimately disagreed, noting that venereal diseases are not typically spread through toilets and that "one would be led to believe that venereal disease would not be expected to occur to any appreciable extent among that segment of the population, whether white or Negro, using the facilities and services afforded by the public libraries of the city."[38] Ultimately, the court ordered Memphis to integrate the library bathrooms under the Fourteenth Amendment's equal protection clause.[39]

The Civil Rights Act of 1964 added statutory protections against racial segregation in public accommodations.[40] But, court cases dealing with racially segregated bathrooms continued into the 1970s, after the Civil Rights Act had outlawed this practice.[41] So, depending on the specific place a Black person lived or worked, they very well may have encountered illegally segregated bathroom facilities long after the federal government deemed this a violation of their civil rights.

Other racial and ethnic minorities have sometimes experienced bathroom exclusion on the basis of their color, although more unevenly as compared to the more all-encompassing Jim Crow system. In *Hernandez v. Texas*, 347 U.S. 475 (1954), the Supreme Court established that Mexican Americans were considered a protected class under the Fourteenth Amendment (at least in some parts of the country), in part due to evidence that Mexican American men at a county courthouse in Texas were required to use a segregated toilet. In another example, a Kansas school district maintained a "tri-racial" segregated school

---

Quarterly 62, no. 1 (2003): 62–63; V. T. Blossom, *It has happened here* (New York: Harper, 1959), 40–43.

[36] Godfrey, "Bayonets," 59–64.

[37] W. A. Wiegand and S. A. Wiegand, *The desegregation of public libraries in the Jim Crow south: Civil rights and local activism* (Baton Rouge: Louisiana State University Press, 2018), 70–73.

[38] *Turner v. Randolph*, 195 F. Supp. 677 (W.D. Tenn. 1961), 680.

[39] *Turner v. Randolph*, 195 F. Supp. 677 (W.D. Tenn. 1961).

[40] Civil Rights Act of 1964, Public Law 88-352, 78 Stat. 241.

[41] See, for example, *James v. Stockham Valves and Fittings Co.*, 559 F.2d 310 (1977).

system for Black, white, and Mexican students, with the Mexican school's students having access to only "toilet facilities of the poorest and worst type ... poorly constructed outdoor privies which were infested with flies" through the 1940s.[42] Native people faced bathroom segregation in some times and places, too. For example, Malinda Maynor Lowery recalls her father, a North Carolina factory worker and member of the Lumbee Tribe, encountering bathrooms segregated as "White, Indian, and Colored," although he was only required to use the "Indian" restroom at certain times of the day.[43]

2.2 The Origins of Sex-Segregated Restrooms

Racially segregated bathrooms were first legally mandated in the 1880s, and during that same period, another policy regulating who could use which bathrooms also began to appear in statute books: sex-segregated bathrooms began to be legislated upon for the first time. While public urination and two-person, non-gendered privies were once seen as normal, demands for privacy based on sex began to become more culturally and politically relevant during this period.[44] As women began to more commonly enter the public sphere and workplace – especially factories – legislators enacted laws requiring separate toilet facilities for women. Massachusetts was the first state to do so, in 1887. The act's title focused on "secur[ing] proper sanitary provisions in factories and workshops," and laid out requirements for "water-closets, earth-closets, or privies" in these locations. Among the requirements were that if a factory or workshop employed both men and women, the employer was required to provide separate facilities with clear signage and "no person shall be allowed to use any such closet or privy assigned to persons of the other sex."[45] By 1920, this type of policy had spread to forty-three other states.[46]

Although these statutes often began as workplace regulations, Terry Kogan argues that they were not motivated solely or primarily by a desire to create safer and healthier factories but by "deep social anxieties over women leaving their homes – their appropriate 'separate sphere' – to enter the work force."[47]

---

[42] J. F. Laird, "Argentine, Kansas: The evolution of a Mexican American community, 1905–1940" (PhD Thesis University of Kansas, 1975), 195–196.

[43] M. M. Lowery, *Lumbee Indians in the Jim Crow south: Race, identity, and the making of a nation* (Chapel Hill: The University of North Carolina Press, 2010), 121–122.

[44] P. C. Baldwin, "Public privacy: Restrooms in American cities, 1869–1932," *Journal of Social History* 48, no. 2 (2014): 267.

[45] Massachusetts Acts & Resolves, Ch. 103, "An Act to secure proper sanitary provisions in factories and workshops" (1887).

[46] T. S. Kogan, "Public restrooms and the distorting of transgender identity," *North Carolina Law Review* 95, no. 4 (2016): 1214–1215.

[47] T. S. Kogan, "Sex separation: The cure-all for Victorian social anxiety," in *Toilet: Public restrooms and the politics of sharing*, ed. H. Molotch and L. Noren (New York: New York University Press, 2010), 145–164.

Kogan argues that male politicians responded to these anxieties in part through requiring separate bathrooms. These separate bathrooms would serve four interrelated purposes: protecting women's bodies – perceived as vulnerable and weak – from dangerous public spaces; the belief that sex-separated spaces would be more sanitary and cleanly; unease around modesty when women were engaged in "intimate bodily functions;" and finally ideas about social morality that viewed sex separation as necessary from a moral perspective to preserve domestic womanhood as distinctive and valued.[48] We see some of these same arguments in discussions of sex-segregated bathrooms today – both in concerns about privacy, but also arguments that cisgender women are especially vulnerable in bathrooms and thus need spaces segregated on the basis of sex assigned at birth to remain safe and protected.

Over time, all-male workplaces and educational institutions used the absence of women's restrooms and the requirement that bathrooms be sex-segregated as an excuse for excluding women from those spaces all together. Judith Plaskow highlights Yale Medical School, Harvard Law School, the Virginia Military Institute (VMI), and the Bronx and Brooklyn Bar Association as all making this type of argument – that the architectural choices that had been made in building historically all-male spaces simply made it impossible to admit women.[49] For example, VMI leadership argued that its physical spaces – in particular open showers and a lack of doors on toilet stalls in the dorms – could not provide adequate privacy to potential future female cadets.[50] After the Supreme Court ordered VMI to begin admitting women in 1996 and the school began to remodel its buildings to allow for separate sex facilities, male administrators insisted on modifications to accommodate women's "special hygienic needs" and to avoid risks of "blood pathogens" from menstruating women.[51]

Relatedly, calls for gender equality in bathrooms have sometimes focused on the idea of "potty parity." This term refers to the issue of unequal, inadequate, and/or missing women's bathrooms in the context of sex-segregated bathrooms.[52] Even when men's restrooms and women's restrooms are of equal size, women typically face longer lines and wait times for both biological and cultural reasons.[53]

---

[48] T. S. Kogan, "Sex-separation in public restrooms: Law, architecture, and gender," *Michigan Journal of Gender & Law* 14, no. 1 (2007): 54.

[49] Plaskow, "Embodiment."

[50] L. F. Brodie, *Breaking out: VMI and the coming of women* (New York: Pantheon Books, 2000), 106.

[51] Brodie, *Breaking out*, 113.

[52] K. H. Anthony and M. Dufresne, "Potty privileging in perspective: Gender and family issues," in *Ladies and gents: Public toilets and gender*, ed. O. Gershenson and B. Penner (Philadelphia: Temple University Press, 2009), 50–51.

[53] C. Greed, "Creating a nonsexist restroom," in *Toilet: Public restrooms and the politics of sharing*, ed. H. Molotch and L. Noren (New York: New York University Press, 2010), 118; H.

Potty parity legislation, passed in twenty-four states and many more cities beginning in the 1980s, aims to address these disparities by mandating specific ratios of fixtures in men's and women's bathrooms.[54] Ratios vary, but common requirements are 2:1 or 3:2 ratios for toilets in women's restrooms versus men's restrooms to account for women's greater time usage needs in toilet stalls.[55]

2.3 Public Toilets and Pay Toilets

The Progressive Era – typically defined as around 1890 through the 1920s – was a period of US history defined by broad social and political activism focused on a wide range of reforms. Among other social and demographic changes that Progressive Era reformers were responding to was growing urbanization – cities were getting bigger, denser, and more populated, along with all the problems that came with those changes. One of the targets of Progressive Era advocacy was the building of public bathrooms – also called comfort stations – in US cities, especially in the Northeast and Midwest.[56] Those comfort stations that were built in the South were typically racially segregated.[57]

To some extent, this movement was the result of technological change – the developments in plumbing and urban infrastructure necessary to build such structures were emerging just before and during the Progressive Era.[58] But reformers pointed to many benefits of public bathrooms. A major one was public health, with a focus on sanitation and cleanliness, especially as urban populations grew and moral concerns about the urban poor developed.[59] Public bathrooms were also linked to the temperance movement, which opposed alcohol and advocated for Prohibition. When public bathrooms weren't available, saloons were the major place that people – in particular men – could relieve themselves while out in the city and not near their home. Public comfort stations provided an alternative, where one could use a toilet without buying a beer.[60]

Women's groups were some of the most active in the areas of both public health and temperance, and they were major advocates of urban public restrooms. Despite their activism around these issues, many more facilities were built for men than for women, and promised construction of women's facilities

---

F. Davis, "Why the 'transgender' bathroom controversy should make us rethink sex-segregated public bathrooms," *Politics, Groups, and Identities* 6, no. 2 (2018): 210–211; Davis, *Bathroom battlegrounds*, 109.

[54] Anthony and Dufresne, "Potty privileging," 56–57; Davis, *Bathroom battlegrounds*, 44.

[55] W. T. Huh, J. Lee, H. Park, and K. S. Park, "The potty parity problem: Towards gender equality at restrooms in business facilities," *Socio-Economic Planning Sciences* 68 (2019), 1–10.

[56] Baldwin, "Public privacy."   [57] Baldwin, "Public privacy," 277.

[58] Baldwin, "Public privacy," 267, 273.

[59] R. Colker, "Public restrooms: Flipping the default rules," *Ohio State Law Journal* 78, no. 1 (2017): 153–154.

[60] Colker, "Public restrooms," 155.

often stalled out. In her research on public toilets in Chicago, for example, Maureen Flanagan finds that women organized extensively around the issue of public toilets but ultimately "male-controlled municipal authorities worked to preserve the city for men's benefit by denying women's claim for more access to public space."[61] This meant the construction of more public toilets designated for use by men, and fewer or no public toilets designated for use by women.

At the movement's height in 1919, almost one hundred cities operated at least one public restroom or comfort station.[62] Over time, though, upper- and middle-class white women – major groups involved in reform efforts – began to rely more heavily on bathrooms located in private businesses when they were out in public, in places like department stores and hotels. These bathrooms of course weren't accessible to lower-class women, but provided amenities that wealthier women valued, like more space, lounges and sofas, and design elements to remind them of home.[63] This shift, as well as growing costs, led to a decline in the truly public, government-provided restroom.[64] Public restrooms became less common and less well-maintained, and people started to think of bathroom provision as less the responsibility of the government and more something that would be provided to customers of businesses.[65]

Still, there have been other significant programs focused on the provision of public bathrooms after the comfort station era. In the 1930s, Roosevelt's New Deal program included the construction of both public and private bathrooms largely in rural areas and often in public parks, through government agencies like the Works Progress Administration and Civil Works Administration.[66] And after WWII, with increased reliance on cars and the growth of the interstate system, public "rest stops" along highways that included toilet facilities became increasingly common.[67] In recent years, some cities have begun pilot projects to

---

[61] M. Flanagan, "Private needs, public space: Public toilets provision in the Anglo-Atlantic patriarchal city: London, Dublin, Toronto and Chicago," *Urban History* 41, no. 2 (2014): 266.

[62] Baldwin, "Public privacy," 276.

[63] Baldwin, "Public privacy," 272, 278–279; Weinmeyer, "Lavatories," 411–412.

[64] Weinmeyer, "Lavatories," 411–412; Baldwin, "Public privacy," 279.

[65] Baldwin, "Public privacy," 281; Colker, "Public restrooms," 157; Banks, "Disappearing public toilet," 1067.

[66] E. S. Tisdale and C. H. Atkins, "The sanitary privy and its relation to public health," *American Journal of Public Health and the Nation's Health* 33, no. 11 (1943): 1319–1322; D. Wolfenbarger, New Deal resources on Colorado's eastern plains, (NPS Form 10-900-b: National Register of Historic Places Multiple Property Documentation Form: United States Department of the Interior – National Parks Service, 2005); E. Yuko, "Where did all the public bathrooms go?" *Bloomberg*, November 5, 2021, www.bloomberg.com/news/features/2021-11-05/why-american-cities-lost-their-public-bathrooms.

[67] Yuko, "Public bathrooms."; J. Liversedge, "Rest areas: Intersections of the American experience" (MA Thesis University of Michigan-Flint, 2022).

survey needs and begin to install more public restrooms, although these efforts ultimately fall short of meeting the full needs of the public.[68]

A final category of quasi-public toilets is the pay toilet, which is relatively common in Europe but often illegal in the United States.[69] Pay toilets, which require a small fee to use, first appeared at the 1893 World's Fair and were popularized in the 1930s.[70] By their height in the 1970s, pay toilets were a "$30 million-a-year industry" and there were around 50,000 of them installed around the country.[71] Around this time, however, opposition to pay toilets began to grow, first through locally organized groups and then growing to broader activism, especially from women's groups.[72] Women argued that pay toilets discriminated against them because men could typically use free urinals, while they had no choice but to pay for a toilet in a stall.[73] Primarily in the 1970s and 1980s, although continuing through the 2000s, eighteen states passed legislation either banning paid toilets or restricting their use.[74] Whether legislatively prohibited or not, independently operated pay toilets have largely disappeared from the United States.

2.4 Federalism and Social Citizenship

Across multiple identities, it is clear that toilet access has been a key component of social citizenship throughout US history, and restricting access to bathrooms has been used to exclude groups both historically and continuing today. The processes by which groups are included or excluded from bathrooms often involve political actors such as lawmakers and judges, but they are not limited to those with government authority. Organized groups clearly play a role as well, such as the upper- and middle-class women's groups that advocated for public restrooms and then dropped the issue from their agenda after a private alternative became more attractive. Even less organized private actors can have significant impacts, especially in the aggregate, as in the example of private employers refusing to comply with civil rights laws.

At the same time, bathroom provision is more nuanced than a simple inclusion-exclusion binary. Sex-segregated bathrooms are an example of this. On the one hand, the provision of women's restrooms is connected to their

---

[68] Weinmeyer, "Lavatories," 430–431; Progressive Urban Management Associates, City of Denver public restrooms pilot project (Denver, 2018).

[69] Banks, "Disappearing public toilet," 1091–1092.

[70] Weinmeyer, "Lavatories," 413; E. Montano, "The bring your own tampon policy: Why menstrual hygiene products should be provided for free in restrooms," *University of Miami Law Review* 73, no. 1 (2018): 375.

[71] Montano, "Bring your own tampon," 372, 375.

[72] Montano, "Bring your own tampon," 379–382.

[73] Montano, "Bring your own tampon," 382.   [74] Weinmeyer, "Lavatories," 416.

growing presence in public spaces, and especially their participation in the workforce. But, the desire for these spaces to be separated by sex reflected perceptions of women as fragile and in need of protection, and unequal provision of women's bathrooms has justified ongoing exclusions.

And, as this account reveals, a large number of policies involving bathroom access are controlled at the state and municipal level. This is because many of these policies fall under the police powers (regulations that impact health, safety, and morals), which are an area of traditional state control under the US Constitution. State and local governments have enacted a wide variety of legislation that has both expanded and contracted Americans' ability to access bathrooms in public spaces and while at work. This means that individuals and groups may experience greater or lesser social citizenship depending on which state – or even which city – they reside in or travel to, a lesson starkly displayed during the Jim Crow era but one that remains true today in other contexts. This, in turn, impacts the ability to fully take part in public life and have full access to opportunities in education, the workforce, and civic life, creating uneven levels of citizenship even where national citizenship remains constant.

In the modern era, J. Mitchell Pickerill and Cynthia J. Bowling identify American federalism as fragmented. By this, they mean that when the national government fails to enact universal policies, "the laws that are passed in states with unified party control often result in polarized policies leading to fractures in the intergovernmental arrangements between states and in federal–state relations."[75] Jake Grumbach describes a related phenomenon, "polarized laboratories of democracy," in which red states rely on one set of interest groups and experts and copy policies from one another, while blue states replicate this process with their own set of resources – leading to bifurcated policy outcomes.[76] This pattern is most clear when it comes to policies impacting trans people's ability to access bathrooms according with their gender identity, with some Republican-led states enacting trans-exclusionary bathroom bills and some Democratic-led states passing laws that explicitly protect bathroom access for trans people.

In other cases, such as laws aimed at increasing access to baby changing tables in men's rooms, polarization is less prevalent, and bipartisanship is more common. For these policies, though, individuals still often face differing levels of bathroom access depending on their location and identity, even if not on the basis of state-level partisanship. Though these policies may often enjoy bipartisan support if they reach a final vote, their enactment still requires state-level

---

[75] J. M. Pickerill and C. J. Bowling, "Polarized parties, politics, and policies: Fragmented federalism in 2013–2014," *Publius: The Journal of Federalism* 44, no. 3 (2014): 369.

[76] J. M. Grumbach, *Laboratories against democracy: How national parties transformed state politics* (Princeton: Princeton University Press, 2022), 11–12.

advocacy and lobbying, as well as policy entrepreneurship on the part of state legislatures who choose to take up specific issues related to bathrooms. The result is uneven implementation across the states.

3 Bathrooms, Gender, and Gender Roles

Because bathrooms in the United States are typically sex-segregated, the physical spaces of bathrooms that are available to the public and what is provided within those spaces are impacted by society's perceptions of gender. For example, is a baby changing table provided only in a women's room – because mothers are assumed to be the ones caring for their children – or can all parents access a changing table? The choices that both private businesses and government make about this design choice has implications for who is comfortable and welcome in a space and, more broadly, how our society views parents and their gendered responsibilities. States have also passed legislation requiring the provision of free menstrual products in specific settings. This section explores their provision in two very different state-controlled institutions: public schools and state prisons. Although policies about changing tables and menstrual products do not involve blocking people from accessing toilet facilities all together, each has important implications for dignity and inclusion, and thus is deeply intertwined with social citizenship.

3.1 Baby Changing Tables in Men's Restrooms

A first bathroom-related policy that connects to issues of gender and gender roles is the inclusion of baby changing tables in bathrooms that are accessible to both men and women. These laws were enacted in two waves, with four states adopting this policy in the 1990s and a further eleven doing so two decades later, in the 2010s and early 2020s. Congress also passed a national version of this law during the second wave, the BABIES Act signed into law in 2016, which requires baby changing tables in both men's and women's restrooms in publicly accessible federal buildings.[77]

There are three broad and sometimes overlapping categories of gender-inclusive baby changing table statutes. The weakest version simply requires gender equity *if* a building has baby changing tables. That is, restrooms need not include baby changing tables at all, but if they do, they must be equally accessible to all genders. This type of law was most common in the first wave, with three states passing this type of regulation in the 1990s (North Carolina, Missouri, and

---

[77] BABIES Act, Public Law 114-235, 130 Stat. 964 (2016). Notably, though, the federal legislation does not apply to congressional office buildings, an issue raised by the Congressional Dads Caucus. J. Kurtz, "Congressional Dads Caucus calls for more baby changing stations in Capitol complex," *The Hill*, April 28, 2023, https://thehill.com/blogs/in-the-know/3978018-congressional-dads-caucus-calls-for-more-baby-changing-stations-in-capitol-complex/.

Michigan) and one in 2022 (Deleware). Another version of this statute is comparable to the federal BABIES Act, requiring that baby changing tables be installed in either men's *and* women's restrooms *or* in gender neutral restrooms, but only in state or municipal buildings and/or buildings built with public funds. Five states – Rhode Island, Colorado, Utah, Arizona, and Maryland – passed this version, all during the second wave of laws except Rhode Island.

Finally, the strongest version of baby changing table legislation requires changing tables in restrooms accessible to all genders in all public accommodations or public restrooms. Although the exact distinction of which specific types of restrooms are covered varies by state, generally this type of law applies to locations such as restaurants, movie theaters, grocery stores, and similar locations that provide public restrooms, in addition to state and local government buildings. Six states – California, Connecticut, Illinois, New Mexico, Nevada, and New York – have enacted this type of statute, all after 2017. Each category of statute is reflected in Figure 1.

Advocacy around baby changing table legislation has ranged from celebrity endorsements to individual advocacy by fathers both inside and outside of government, as well as lobbying by companies with a financial stake in changing tables. Ashton Kutcher made headlines in 2015, making the argument that the inclusion of changing tables in men's rooms was crucial for gender equality: "I would like my daughter to experience a world where gender doesn't dictate one's responsibility or limit one's opportunity . . . Having changing tables in men's rooms is just a tiny step in the process of rectifying legacy gender discrimination."[78] Kutcher's campaign

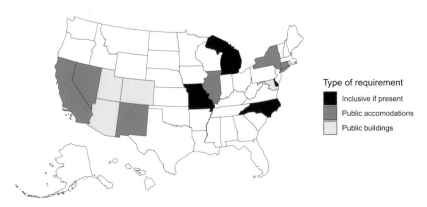

Figure 1 Map of state laws requiring gender-equitable access
to baby changing tables

---

[78] S. Larimer, "Ashton Kutcher just wants to change his kid's diaper, man," *Washington Post*, March 25, 2015, www.washingtonpost.com/news/parenting/wp/2015/03/25/ashton-kutcher-just-wants-to-change-his-kids-diaper-man/.

targeted businesses as opposed to lawmakers, asking large businesses such as Target and Costco to install changing tables in places accessible to all genders.[79]

A few years later, Donte Palmer went "viral" on Instagram after one of his children took a photo of him attempting to change his baby in a men's room that did not have a changing table. He used this attention to encourage other dads to get involved through the hashtag #SquatForChange, referencing the need to squat and change a baby on a parent's lap when appropriate facilities are not available. Palmer emphasized that fathers are caretakers for their children and thus need and deserve changing tables that are accessible to them in public places. Celebrities like John Legend have contributed to the effort, posting their own photos and videos of inadequate changing facilities.[80] This effort has partnered with brands such as Pampers and Koala Kare to fund voluntary installation of changing tables in private businesses.[81]

In turn, the baby changing table company Koala Kare has lobbied lawmakers to require the installation of changing tables, and has worked to organize fathers around this effort, especially on social media.[82] Lawmakers have emphasized both gender equality between mothers and fathers, as well as the needs of same-sex couples in which both parents are men. D.C. Councilmember Brianne K. Nadeau said of a municipal proposal to provide equal access to changing tables: "We introduced this bill during Pride Month and that wasn't by accident."[83]

In addition to equity issues around both gender and sexual orientation, fathers speaking out about changing table access have highlighted sanitation and safety for their babies.[84] And, indeed, research indicates that changing diapers on

---

[79] A. Kutcher, "Change.Org: Stop gender stereotyping: Provide universally accessible changing tables in all your stores," 2015, accessed December 19, 2022, www.change.org/p/bethechange-provide-universally-accessible-changing-tables-in-all-your-stores?utm_source=Aplus&utm_medium=website&utm_campaign=bethechange.

[80] "Squat for change: Photo of dad and baby on floor sparks call for diaper-changing stations in men's restrooms," *ABC13*, October 3, 2018, https://abc13.com/diaper-changing-tables-in-mens-restrooms-squat-for-change/4399279/. L. Bever, "'As if we don't exist': Frustrated father pleads for more changing tables in men's restrooms," *Washington Post*, October 3, 2018, www.washingtonpost.com/news/parenting/wp/2018/10/03/as-if-we-dont-exist-frustrated-father-pleads-for-more-changing-tables-in-mens-restrooms/; "Squat for change," 2022, https://squatforchange.com/.

[81] "Love the change: Pampers, Koala Kare to install 5,000 changing tables in men's restrooms across U.S. and Canada," *ABC7*, June 12, 2019, https://abc7chicago.com/pampers-love-for-change-john-legend-donte-palmer/5343179/.

[82] "Koala Kare: Dads for change," 2022, www.koalabear.com/parent-resources/dads-for-change/.

[83] H. Natanson, "Should there be diaper-changing stations in men's bathrooms? With proposed new law, D.C. wades into national debate," *Washington Post*, July 14, 2019, www.washingtonpost.com/local/social-issues/should-there-be-diaper-changing-stations-in-mens-bathrooms-with-proposed-law-dc-wades-into-national-debate/2019/07/14/72c800f6-9cc8-11e9-85d6-5211733f92c7_story.html.

[84] Natanson, "Diaper-changing stations."

floors, ledges, counters, or other surfaces in bathrooms that are not designed for baby changing can lead to increased risk of infection as well as dangerous falls.[85] Thus a lack of appropriate changing tables can signal exclusion not only for caregivers but of young children themselves. Sometimes this exclusion is appropriate – for example, in nightclubs or other businesses that cater to an adult clientele. Accordingly, some state legislation relating to changing tables acknowledges this and specifically exempts this type of business.[86] But, for public places such as parks and restaurants – and especially government buildings where citizens engage with politics – this exclusion is much more problematic.

Baby changing table legislation focused on gender equity has largely been bipartisan. The BABIES Act passed with bipartisan support in the House and by unanimous consent in the Senate.[87] State legislatures have also tended to pass this legislation in a bipartisan fashion, as indicated in Table 1. Some of the exceptions to this trend are cases where states packaged baby changing table legislation with other policies in broader packages such budget bills or – in the case of Colorado – a requirement to provide more all-gender bathrooms in state buildings. Of the two party unity votes that did focus on the single issue of baby changing tables, both dealt with the most expansive type of policy (covering all public accommodations), and opposition came from Republicans.

Table 1 Final passage votes/floor decisions on gender-equitable baby changing table legislation, 2017–2023

States Enacting Policy, 2017–2023	11
Total Number of Final Passage Floor Decisions	22
Percent Unanimous	41
Percent Party Unity Votes	23

---

[85] N. Pandya, R. Granberg, and M. R. K., "A method for investigating access to diaper changing stations in restaurants," *Cureus* 13, no. 10 (2021): 1–6; A. Rosenberg, *Turning the tables: Requiring access to diaper changing stations* (Madison: Wisconsin Policy Project, 2019).

[86] For example, Illinois' 2019 law specifically excludes "An industrial building, nightclub, or bar that does not permit anyone who is under 18 years of age to enter the premises." Illinois Public Act 101-0293 (2019).

[87] Congress.gov, "Actions overview: H.R.5147 – 114th Congress (2015–2016)," 2016, accessed November 8, 2023, www.congress.gov/bill/114th-congress/house-bill/5147/actions.

3.2 Availability of Menstrual Products in State-Controlled Restrooms

Activist Jennifer Weiss-Wolf coined the term "menstrual equity" in a 2016 interview to describe a growing movement with the core goal of enacting policies to "ensure menstrual products are safe and affordable and available to those who need them."[88] Weiss-Wolf's discussion of menstrual equity echoes core components of social citizenship: "the ability to access [menstrual products] affects a person's freedom to work and study, to be healthy, and to participate in daily life with dignity."[89] Other scholars emphasize similar themes, especially around dignity. Elizabeth Cooper, for example, writes that the deeply personal and physical nature of menstruation means that related policies send messages to individuals about dignity and belongingness: the "ability to manage [menstruation] safely and affordably affects our ability to engage fully with the external world."[90]

Menstrual equity policy issues are wide-ranging, including statutes that eliminate the sales tax on period products and efforts focused on the safety and environmental impact of these products.[91] One set of policies that falls under menstrual equity and has particular relevance for this Element is the provision of free menstrual products in certain bathrooms that are owned and operated by state entities. Specifically, these laws have focused on providing menstrual products in public schools and in correctional facilities (illustrated in Figure 2). Although menstruation of course happens outside of bathrooms, bathrooms are one of the main places that people

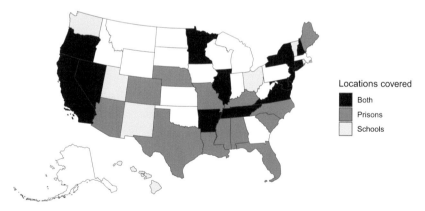

Figure 2 Map of state laws requiring provision of menstrual products in state-controlled institutional settings

---

[88] J. Weiss-Wolf, *Periods gone public: Taking a stand for menstrual equity* (New York: Arcade, 2017), xvi.

[89] Weiss-Wolf, *Periods gone public*, xvi.

[90] E. B. Cooper, "What's law got to do with it? Dignity and menstruation," *Columbia Journal of Gender and Law* 41 (2021): 41.

[91] A. Crays, "Menstrual equity and justice in the United States," *Sexuality, Gender, and Policy* 3 (2020): 134–147.

manage menstruation, and the sex-segregated nature of many public bathrooms and correctional institutions means that choices about where and how to provide menstrual products in bathrooms is closely connected to issues of gender.

It is important to note here that the need for menstrual products is not limited to women's bathrooms. As Weiss-Wolf notes, the discussion of gender and gender identity with regard to menstrual equity is complicated "given that the vast majority of people who have periods are cisgender women and girls, as well as that so much of menstrual taboo is rooted in ages-old misogyny. Ultimately, though, everyone and anyone who menstruates needs to be included in discussions and decisions about their own health."[92] Interviews with trans and non-binary people who menstruate indicated that public bathroom design and a lack of available products and disposal options in men's restrooms negatively impacted their feelings of safety and increased the risk of harassment.[93] As I discuss below, some state legislation explicitly excludes trans and non-binary people who menstruate, while other states explicitly address the needs of this population.

Advocacy efforts around menstrual equity have intentionally framed the issue around "equity and civic participation" as opposed to sanitation and public health.[94] As Amy Fettig puts it, beyond specific policy goals, the menstrual equity movement much more broadly seeks to "root out the structures that undermine the full participation of people who menstruate in society at large."[95] And indeed, many states have explicitly included references to dignity in their legislation's titles or text, such as Illinois' "Learn with Dignity Act" and Mississippi's "Dignity for Incarcerated Women Act."[96]

Despite an advocacy focus on dignity and equity, these policies also do have important consequences for public health. In the school context, a lack of access to appropriate menstrual products has been linked to high rates of absenteeism as well as higher risks of "reproductive tract infections, urinary tract infections, and increased spread of sexually transmitted diseases," especially among low-income students.[97] Thus, even though an absence of no-cost period products

---

[92] Weiss-Wolf, *Periods gone public*, xviii.

[93] B. Lane, A. Perez-Brumer, R. Parker, A. Sprong, and M. Sommer, "Improving menstrual equity in the USA: Perspectives from trans and non-binary people assigned female at birth and health care providers," *Culture, Health & Sexuality* 24, no. 10 (2022): 1408–1422.

[94] J. Weiss-Wolf, "U.S. Policymaking to address menstruation: Advancing an equity agenda," in *The Palgrave handbook of critical menstruation studies*, ed. C. Bobel, I. T. Winkler, B. Fahs, et al. (Palgrave MacMillan, 2020), 539.

[95] A. Fettig, "Menstrual equity, organizing and the struggle for human dignity and gender equality in prison," *Columbia Journal of Gender and Law* 41 (2021): 79–80.

[96] Illinois Public Act 100-0163 (2017) and Mississippi HB 196 (2021).

[97] L. Francis, S. Meraj, D. Konduru, and E. M. Perrin, "An update on state legislation supporting menstrual hygiene products in US schools: A legislative review, policy report, and recommendations for school nurse leadership," *The Journal of School Nursing* (2023): 1.

doesn't absolutely exclude menstruating students from schools, the practical effect may be that those students are not willing to come to school if they don't have the ability to safely manage menstruation while there. Meanwhile, in prisons, incarcerated women without adequate access to period products will often wear tampons for longer than recommended or resort to homemade products, increasing their risk of toxic shock syndrome and other infections.[98]

As with some other bathroom-related policies, experimentation began with local government. In 2016, New York City was the first US city to enact a comprehensive policy related to menstrual equity, which included the provision of free menstrual products in schools and correctional facilities, as well as homeless shelters.[99] Importantly, the New York City policy focused on the provision of products in school *bathrooms* as opposed to distributing them through nurses or other adult gatekeepers.[100] This allowed students to access products in less time and with less risk of embarrassment, and smaller pilot programs in the city demonstrated that there was high student demand for period products and that they were not misused at unacceptable rates.[101] And, the policy worked – school attendance rose after implementation.[102] This data suggests that while the absence of policies around free menstrual products does not entirely exclude menstruating students from school, a substantial number of students – especially low-income students – may self-exclude when they do not have confidence that they will be able to meet their menstrual needs with dignity. Following New York City's experience, menstrual equity policies quickly became popular with both state governments as well as, to a more limited extent, the federal government.

Turning first to policies focused on prisons and jails, twenty-seven states and the federal government have enacted laws that require correctional facilities to provide menstrual products to inmates who need them. The federal policy – passed as part of the First Step Act in 2018 – applies to inmates in federal prisons. Among many other criminal justice reforms, it requires that federal prisons provide tampons and pads to inmates who need them, for free. The language in the federal statute is gender neutral, but does not explicitly reference trans and non-binary inmates.[103]

Like the federal government, states began to adopt menstrual equity statutes in 2018, with most state laws (about 96 percent) applying to state prisons, more than

---

[98] Fettig, "Menstrual equity," 86; S. Darivemula, A. Knittel, L. Flowers, et al., "Menstrual equity in the criminal legal system," *Journal of Women's Health* 32, no. 9 (2023): 927–931.

[99] M. L. Schmitt, K. Booth, and M. Sommer, "A policy for addressing menstrual equity in schools: A case study from New York City, U.S.A.," *Frontiers in Reproductive Health* 3 (2022): 2.

[100] Schmitt, Booth, and Sommer, "Menstrual equity," 4.

[101] Schmitt, Booth, and Sommer, "Menstrual equity," 4.

[102] Montano, "Bring your own tampon," 404.

[103] First Step Act of 2018, Public Law 115–391, 132 Stat. 5194.

half (63 percent) applying to county and local jails, and only one state – Colorado – extending its policy to private prisons in the state. Twenty-one states specify that menstrual products must be provided at no cost to the inmate, and the remaining simply state that they must be made available to inmates or that products only need to be provided for free to indigent inmates. Finally, about three-quarters of state laws use gender-specific language and require the provision of products only to female inmates or in correctional institutions that house women. The remaining quarter use gender neutral language such as "all committed persons who menstruate."[104] Colorado's law specifically references the fact that "[p]eople in jail custody who are women, transgender, or nonbinary encounter different challenges than men while incarcerated."[105]

Turning to educational settings, state menstrual equity statutes impacting schools were first passed in 2017. By the end of the 2023 legislative session, twenty-two states had passed laws requiring menstrual products in at least some schools, while an additional seven states started grant programs to provide period products in schools or included at least some funding in the state budget for the provision of these products. I focus my analysis here on the states that guarantee product provision in either all schools or schools serving primarily low-income populations. Most of these state laws cover K-12 schools with a focus on middle and high schools, and three states – California, Oregon, and Connecticut – extend their mandates to public higher education.

Most state statutes (81 percent) specify that products must be provided in bathrooms as opposed to in a nurses' office or similar locations. Four states require products only in girls' bathrooms, while twelve include some mention of gender inclusivity, and the remaining don't specify either way. An example of gender-inclusive language comes from New Mexico's bill, requiring period products to be provided in "each women's bathroom and gender-neutral bathroom and at least one men's bathroom in every public middle school, junior high school, secondary school and high school."[106] Other states don't mention men's or boys' bathrooms but do reference gender neutral bathrooms.[107] Finally, thirteen states don't identify a specific state funding source, with four states explicitly requiring schools to fund the provision of period products through their own budget or through donations. Vermont, for example, includes a provision stating: "School districts and approved independent schools shall bear the cost of supplying menstrual products and may seek grants or partner with a nonprofit or community-based organization to fulfill this obligation."[108]

---

[104] Illinois Public Act 102-1111 (2022).   [105] Colorado Session Laws Ch. 131 (2019).
[106] New Mexico HB 134 (2023).   [107] See, for example, New Hampshire SB 142 (2019).
[108] Vermont Legislature Act 66 (2021).

Table 2 Final passage votes/floor decisions on statutes requiring free provision of menstrual products in prisons

States Enacting Policy, 2018–2023	27
Total Number of Final Floor Decisions	53
Percent Unanimous	79
Percent Party Unity Votes (Excludes Nebraska)	4

Multiple scholars have pointed out that menstrual equity bills tend to enjoy bipartisan support.[109] This is much more true for legislation aimed at the provision of period products in prisons; the evidence for school-based programs is more mixed. As is evident from Table 2, almost 80 percent of final passage decisions on menstrual equity policies focused on prisons were unanimous (either unanimous roll calls or voice votes/decisions by unanimous consent), and only 4 percent were party unity votes. This is echoed at the federal level, with the First Step Act passing the Senate with unanimous consent, the House with a voice vote, and then being signed by a Republican president.[110]

One reason for bipartisan support for menstrual equity bills relating to correctional facilities may be that both progressive and conservative interest groups have lobbied for their passage. The American Legislative Exchange Council (ALEC) is a conservative, business-oriented group that writes and shares model legislation that is then distributed to state legislatures and – often – adopted.[111] Unsurprisingly, ALEC's model bills relating to prisons and criminal justice are largely focused on "promoting greater use of private prisons, goods, and services … [and] prison labor" as well as "increasing the size of the prison population."[112] But, ALEC also finalized a model bill titled

---

[109] B. J. Crawford, M. E. Johnson, M. L. Karin, L. Strausfeld, and E. G. Waldman, "The ground on which we all stand: A conversation about menstrual equity law and activism," *Michigan Journal of Gender & Law* 26, no. 2 (2019): 374; Weiss-Wolf, "U.S. Policymaking to address menstruation: Advancing an equity agenda," 545.

[110] Congress.gov, "Actions overview: S.756 – 115th Congress (2017–2018)," 2018, accessed November 10, 2023, www.congress.gov/bill/115th-congress/senate-bill/756/actions.

[111] A. Hertel-Fernandez, "Who passes business's 'model bills'? Policy capacity and corporate influence in US state politics," *Perspectives on Politics* 12, no. 3 (2014): 582–602. ALEC also compiles research for state lawmakers about policy successes in other states, providing evidence that can then be used to support the passage of their preferred statutes. See Grumbach, *Laboratories*, 131–132.

[112] R. Cooper, C. Heldman, A. R. Ackerman, and V. A. Farrar-Meyers, "Hidden corporate profits in the US prison system: The unorthodox policy-making of the American Legislative Exchange Council," *Contemporary Justice Review* 19, no. 3 (2016): 387.

Table 3 Final passage votes/floor decisions on statutes requiring free provision of menstrual products in schools

States Enacting Policy, 2018–2023	21
Total Number of Final Floor Decisions	38
Percent Unanimous	43
Percent Party Unity Votes	38
Percent Party Unity Votes: Gender Inclusive Statutes Only	38

"Dignity for Incarcerated Women" in 2018 that includes a number of topics relating to incarcerated women's rights, including a menstrual equity provision requiring the provision of free menstrual products to incarcerated women with financial need.[113] Based on a comparison of the language used, it is clear that the menstrual equity bills adopted in Texas, Arizona, Mississippi, and North Carolina were based at least in part on the ALEC model bill, and of course other states may have taken inspiration from it.[114] More progressive groups like the American Civil Liberties Union (ACLU) are also engaged in advocacy on this issue, sometimes led by formerly incarcerated women, and they offer their own model legislation.[115]

When examining mandates to provide menstrual products in schools, however, states have been more divided (see Table 3). Many (43 percent) of state legislative chambers did vote to enact these policies unanimously. However, a similar proportion of votes (38 percent) were party unity votes, with a majority of Democrats supporting the policy and a majority of Republicans opposed (the exception is Ohio, where the menstrual equity measure was part of a Republican-backed budget bill that Democrats opposed). Lucine Francis and coauthors also found that states controlled by Democrats were more likely to both introduce and pass school-related menstrual equity legislation.[116]

---

[113] American Legislative Exchange Council, "Dignity for incarcerated women," 2018, accessed November 27, 2023, https://alec.org/model-policy/dignity-for-incarcerated-women/.

[114] Texas HB 650 (2019), Arizona SB 1849 (2021), Mississippi HB 196 (2021), North Carolina HB 608 (2021).

[115] K. Haven, "Why I'm fighting for menstrual equity in prison," *ACLU News & Commentary*, November 8, 2019, www.aclu.org/news/prisoners-rights/why-im-fighting-for-menstrual-equity-in-prison; ACLU National Prison Project, *Menstrual equity: A legislative toolkit*, (American Civil Liberties Union, 2019), www.aclu.org/wp-content/uploads/legal-documents/121119-sj-periodequitytoolkit.pdf. See also Fettig, "Menstrual equity."

[116] Francis, Meraj, Konduru, and Perrin, "An update on state legislation supporting menstrual hygiene products in US schools."

While some of the party unity votes in this data can be explained because the measure was part of a broader bill covering multiple topics, this is not a clear pattern. I also examined whether the partisan differences might be the result of some bills being more inclusive of trans and non-binary students, while others limit the provision of menstrual products to girls' bathrooms. But, the rate of party unity votes was similar for gender identity-inclusive legislation. And, at the national level, federal legislation has thus far fizzled out.[117]

One major issue with both school- and prison-focused menstrual equity bills is that of implementation and compliance. Bridget Crawford, for example, discusses how after the passage of New York City's policy, a Girl Scout troop visited schools in Brooklyn and found that only 18 percent were fully compliant.[118] Although the Department of Education responded, promising greater oversight, it remains unclear the extent to which the city and now state policy is fully followed.[119] These types of implementation and oversight challenges are, of course, not unique to New York. Most menstrual equity laws simply require that products be provided without much detail on how compliance will be monitored.[120] And even if state-run institutions try to comply with new requirements, they may provide poor-quality products or interpret laws differently.[121] Kimberly Haven, a director with Reproductive Justice Inside, recommends that local groups monitor compliance through public records requests, but such a strategy is resource-intensive and geographically inconsistent.[122]

---

[117] See, for example, the Menstrual Equity for All Act, introduced by Rep. Grace Meng. Congress. gov, "H.R.3646 – Menstrual Equity For All Act of 2023," 2023, accessed November 7, 2023, www.congress.gov/bill/118th-congress/house-bill/3646. See also R. H. Lerner, "Recognizing menstrual equity as a dimension of equal educational opportunity," *Journal of Law & Education* 52, no. 1 (2023): 252.

[118] Crawford, Johnson, Karin, Strausfeld, and Waldman, "Ground on which," 368.

[119] Schmitt, Booth, and Sommer, "Menstrual equity," 7.

[120] Maryland is an exception, with a fairly detailed oversight procedure for its menstrual equity law covering correctional facilities. See Maryland HB 797 (2018).

[121] Missouri Appleseed, *Research summary: Access to menstrual hygiene products in Missouri prisons* (2023), https://missouriappleseed.org/wp-content/uploads/2023/06/23_MoApp_Menstrual-Hyg-Research.pdf; Haven, "Why I'm fighting for menstrual equity in prison."; M. Vishniac, "The prison flow project," 2023, accessed November 27, 2023, https://theprisonflowproject.com/state-laws-around-access/. See also M. Vishniac, "The new correctional afterthought: Menstruation and incarceration in the U.S.A" (PhD Thesis University of Edinburgh, 2024), https://era.ed.ac.uk/.

[122] ACLU National Prison Project, *Menstrual equity: A legislative toolkit*, 23.

4 Bathrooms and Gender Identity

In recent years, states and municipalities have implemented policies aimed at both restricting and expanding bathroom access for trans people and others who do not fit neatly within the gender binary. So-called "bathroom bills" are the most prominent bathroom-related policy covered in the news today. These laws aim to limit access to sex-segregated bathrooms based on the sex listed on an individual's original birth certificate or some other measure of "biological sex." Most states that have enacted these laws have done so in ways that especially target trans youth in public schools.

Bathroom access policies focused on gender identity are part of a new and concerted focus in state law on trans people's social citizenship that impacts many aspects of daily life. State-level legislation targeting trans people has been increasing dramatically in recent years, going beyond bathroom access to include bans on youth participation in sports, restrictions on discussions of gender identity in schools, requirements that schools "out" trans students to parents against their wishes, restrictions on identity documents for trans and gender non-conforming people, and restrictions on gender affirming health care.[123] Yet, while the specific targets of these laws may be newer, the strategy of limiting access to public spaces and schools through restrictive bathroom policies is part of the longer legacy of bathroom policy that aims to exclude certain groups from full social citizenship.

In contrast, other states and municipalities have enacted policies that aim to increase or ensure access for trans and gender non-conforming people. In these places, easy access to bathrooms sends messages to trans and gender non-conforming people that they are full and equal members of society. One of the easiest and least controversial policies in this vein is a requirement that all single-stall bathrooms be labelled as gender neutral and thus available to any individual. More comprehensive are laws and policies that include explicit non-discrimination protections based on gender identity, including in the use of sex-segregated bathrooms.

It is important to note at the outset that this area of the law has seen substantial judicial activity in recent years. The legality of both trans-exclusionary bathroom bills and gender-inclusive policies – as they relate to multi-user facilities – remains unsettled. State and federal courts around the country have ruled in opposite directions on issues of bathroom access for trans people in cases that deal with employment, public accommodations, and K-12 schools.[124] As of the writing of

---

[123] A. Branigin and N. Kirkpatrick, "Anti-trans laws are on the rise. Here's a look at where – and what kind," *Washington Post*, October 14, 2022, www.washingtonpost.com/lifestyle/2022/10/14/anti-trans-bills/.

[124] In addition to numerous conflicting state and lower federal court decisions on this issue, federal circuit courts have also split in their rulings. The Fourth Circuit ruled in favor of a trans student's right to access the bathroom in accordance with his gender identity in 2020 in *Gavin Grimm v.*

this Element, the Supreme Court has yet to weigh in on this issue. In *Bostock v. Clayton County*, 590 U.S. ___ (2020), the Court found that anti-discrimination policies that prohibit discrimination on the basis of sex can be interpreted to include discrimination on the basis of gender identity. But, the Court explicitly chose not to decide the issue of sex-segregated bathroom facilities under Title VII of the Civil Rights Act.[125] Writing for the majority, Justice Neil Gorsuch states: "we do not purport to address bathrooms, locker rooms, or anything else of the kind."[126] The next year, in 2021, the Court denied cert for a case that would have directly addressed the issue of bathroom access for trans students in K-12 schools.[127]

In addition to the legal activity around this topic, issues of access to bathrooms for trans people have been the subject of a large amount of state- and federal-level bureaucratic rule-making and guidance. While the focus of this Element is on state legislatures and state laws, this issue area in particular is one in which both courts and bureaucratic agencies play a major ongoing role. I will touch on some of these policies and decisions in the analysis below, and it may be the case that legal rulings in the future will bring more uniformity to policies in the coming years.

4.1 Trans-Exclusionary "Bathroom Bills"

Probably the most politically contentious bathroom-related legislation of the past two decades is the introduction and enactment of statutes aimed at restricting access to public bathrooms for transgender people. So-called "bathroom bills" typically restrict access to sex-segregated bathrooms on the basis of "biological sex," often defined as the sex listed on an individual's original birth certificate but sometimes also including chromosomes, genetics, anatomy, and/or reproductive capacity.[128] Numerous states have introduced bathroom bill legislation, and ten have actually enacted these laws, the majority (60 percent) in 2023.

North Carolina's HB2 was both the first bathroom bill to be passed and subject to the most public controversy. Passed in 2016 by a Republican-controlled

---

    Gloucester County School Board, No. 19-1952 (2020) and the Eleventh Circuit ruled in favor of a school district with a trans-exclusive bathroom policy in 2022 in *Drew Adams v. School Board of St. Johns County, Florida,* No. 1813592 (2022).

[125] *Bostock v. Clayton County* 590 U.S. ___ (2020).

[126] *Bostock v. Clayton County* 590 U.S. ___ (2020), 31.

[127] H. Natanson, "Virginia school board will pay $1.3 million in settlement to transgender student Gavin Grimm, who sued over bathroom policy," *Washington Post,* August 26, 2021, www .washingtonpost.com/local/education/transgender-bathroom-settlement-gavin-grimm/2021/ 08/26/0f186784-0699-11ec-a266-7c7fe02fa374_story.html.

[128] See, for example, Florida Statutes sec. 553.865, "Safety in Private Spaces Act" for a definition based on reproductive capacity, and Tennessee Acts (2021), ch. 452, sec. 3, "Accommodations for All Children Act" for a definition based on anatomy, genetics, and original birth certificate.

legislature and signed by Republican governor Pat McCrory, the statute required public schools and government buildings to restrict access to sex-segregated bathrooms based on sex as listed on an individual's birth certificate. This therefore forced trans people to either use a bathroom inconsistent with their gender identity, violate the policy, or avoid multi-stall bathrooms in publicly owned and controlled buildings all together.[129] There was a substantial backlash to the law, including letters from the Justice Department, lawsuits, and boycotts. Ultimately, North Carolina's legislature partially repealed HB2 in 2017, eliminating the restriction on bathroom access by trans people in publicly owned buildings.[130]

By 2021, journalist Katelyn Burns declared that "the bathroom bill era is over" – it was an idea whose time had come and gone, and conservatives had moved on to attacking trans people in other ways.[131] But, since then, bathroom bill legislation has not only returned but accelerated. Kimberly Martin and Elizabeth Rahilly argue that although North Carolina's experience initially led to hesitance among Republican lawmakers in passing similar legislation, Joe Biden's election changed their calculus. In 2021, the Biden administration issued an executive order and other guidance reversing Donald Trump's anti-trans policies and prohibiting schools from discriminating on the basis of gender identity. The issue of trans girls participating in sports got particular traction among politicians and voters, and success in leveraging this issue inspired a new wave of legislation attacking trans people from multiple angles, including in public accommodations.[132]

The more recent wave of bathroom bill legislation falls into a few categories. All states that enacted bathroom bills in 2021-2023 – nine in total – target trans youth in K-12 public (and sometimes charter) schools by requiring that school bathrooms be separated by "biological sex" and that trans students – if they are to be accommodated at all – be forced to use alternate, single-user facilities. Smaller numbers of laws impact bathroom access in higher education (two states), corrections facilities (two states), and public or government buildings (one state).

---

[129] B. S. Barnett, A. E. Nesbit, and R. M. Sorrentino, "The transgender bathroom debate at the intersection of politics, law, ethics, and science," *The Journal of the American Academy of Psychiatry and the Law* 46, no. 2 (2018): 232.

[130] Barnett, Nesbit, and Sorrentino, "Transgender bathroom debate," 232–233. The repeal bill did, however, place limitations on the passage of anti-discrimination ordinances by local governments in the state.

[131] K. Burns, "The bathroom bill era is over," *Medium*, June 30, 2021, https://katelynburns.medium .com/the-bathroom-bill-era-is-over-ed0018b44441. See also D. Ali, "The rise and fall of the bathroom bill: State legislation affecting trans & gender non-binary people," *NASPA, Student Affairs Administrators in Higher Education*, April 2, 2019, www.naspa.org/blog/the-rise-and-fall-of-the-bathroom-bill-state-legislation-affecting-trans-and-gender-non-binary-people.

[132] K. Martin and E. Rahilly, "Value frames in discourse supporting transgender athlete bans," *Discourse & Society* 34, no. 6 (2023): 732–751. On the rise in trans-exclusionary athletics-focused legislation, see also E. A. Sharrow, "Sports, transgender rights and the bodily politics of cisgender supremacy," *Laws* 10, no. 3 (2021): 1–29.

Bathroom bills also vary in terms of enforcement and penalties. Two states do not specify any specific penalty or enforcement mechanism, leading to some local resistance.[133] Of the rest that do, most focus on penalties aimed at the school or school administrator that implements a policy allowing trans students to access bathroom facilities consistent with their gender identity. These penalties include a partial loss of state funding, fines for school employees, and civil liability, often via a private right of action for parents to sue schools if their child encounters a trans person in a bathroom. Florida also imposes penalties on individuals who use bathrooms that are consistent with their gender identity but inconsistent with their biological sex. These can include disciplinary action for prisoners, employees, and students, as well as criminal trespass.[134]

The legality of bathroom bills remains unresolved. In some cases, students and their families have moved out of state after being denied a temporary restraining order, thus protecting the individual student but not allowing potential appeals to move forward.[135] The legal record that does exist points to various violations related to social citizenship, including loss of dignity and access to opportunities. For example, in a case filed in Tennessee, a trans girl developed severe physical and mental health symptoms after being denied equal access to her school bathroom and experiencing bullying at school. Her psychiatrist linked the symptoms to the student's "inability to live her life fully as a girl in all respects, which has been aggravated in particular by her inability to use the girls' restroom at school."[136] As a result, the student was limited in her educational opportunities in part because of the denial of bathroom access. An analysis of amicus briefs in another case revealed similar patterns, with students reporting mental health impacts, lost instructional time, harassment, frequent accidents, and dehydration and other medical consequences when denied bathroom access at school.[137]

Figure 3 illustrates the geography and timing of enacted bathroom bills. As is clear from this map, the passage of these laws is a recent phenomenon. Although the first laws enacted were concentrated in the US South, this type of legislation has become more geographically widespread starting in 2023.

Interest groups have played a significant role in advocating for trans-exclusionary bathroom bills. Although a number of interest groups have supported these laws,

---

[133] J. Dura, J. Hanna, and S. Murphy, "In some states with laws on transgender bathrooms, officials may not know how they will be enforced," *Associated Press*, June 25, 2023, https://apnews .com/article/transgender-bathroom-laws-enforcement-e96e94b8935eb6bd23a42562cdeeec6c.

[134] Florida Statutes, sec. 553.865, "Safety in Private Spaces Act."

[135] *A.S. v. Lee*, 2021 U.S. Dist. LEXIS 146899 (2021). T. Loller, "Transgender child sues over Tennessee school bathroom law," *Associated Press*, August 4, 2022, https://apnews.com/ article/sports-education-lawsuits-tennessee-nashville-e2ec93649389e5b74e191066bd3cd956.

[136] *D.H. v. Williamson Cnty. Bd. of Educ.*, 638 F. Supp. 3d 821, 827 (2022).

[137] Lewis and Eckes, "Storytelling."

Figure 3 Map of trans-exclusionary bathroom legislation
in the United States

the biggest player is the Alliance Defending Freedom (ADF), an Arizona-based conservative legal organization. The ADF developed model legislation focused on limiting bathroom access for trans students in public schools that has been utilized by multiple state legislatures in the drafting process.[138] This model legislation provides for a definition of biological sex based on anatomy at birth; the designation of all public school bathrooms and changing rooms as sex segregated on the basis of this definition of biological sex; and the creation of a private right of action by students who encounter a trans person in a multi-stall bathroom or changing room.[139] We see multiple elements from this model legislation reflected in both proposed and enacted bathroom bills.

All ten states that have enacted bathroom bills specifically addressed bathrooms in K-12 public schools, and the targeting of trans students and youth is particularly important for understanding the context of these laws. This focus is also not unique to bathroom bills. Indeed, as Alison Gash and coauthors note, the use of children as the subject of political debate is prominent throughout US politics, including in battles over LGBT rights.[140] Because children already have fewer civil rights by nature of their age, Jules Gill-Peterson writes that they are "easy

---

[138] M. J. Norton, "Testimony of Michael J. Norton; senior counsel, Alliance Defending Freedom," Alliance Defending Freedom, updated February 14, 2015, accessed June 29, 2022, www.leg .state.co.us/CLICS/CLICS2015A/commsumm.nsf/b4a3962433b52fa787256e5f00670a71/ 4f3a48ec0a54330687257de2005e3f8c/%24FILE/15HouseState0204AttachC.pdf#page=5; S. Michaels, "We tracked down the lawyers behind the recent wave of anti-trans bathroom bills," *Mother Jones*, April 25, 2016, www.motherjones.com/politics/2016/04/alliance-defend ing-freedom-lobbies-anti-lgbt-bathroom-bills/.

[139] Norton, "Testimony of Michael J. Norton."

[140] A. Gash, D. Tichenor, A. Chavez, and M. Musselman, "Framing kids: Children, immigration reform, and same-sex marriage," *Politics, Groups, and Identities* 8, no. 1 (2020): 44–70.

targets for political violence" and in the context of current moral panics over trans rights, anti-trans activists have particularly focused on children because their existence is viewed as "proof that trans life deserves to be repressed in its incipient forms for the threat to the social order that its future would represent."[141] Thus, laws that regulate children's bathroom use shape not only the current environment in schools but also aim to change future social and political landscapes by targeting trans existence among young people.

The presence of trans children in schools is not new – in fact many school districts had been quietly allowing trans students to use bathrooms in accordance with their gender identity prior to the current political backlash around this issue, even in occasional instances as far back as the 1930s.[142] Instead, current battles over bathroom access for trans students are part of "a highly contemporary form of anti–trans backlash that has taken the convergence of trans visibility and vulnerability as an opportunity."[143] It is important to reiterate here that these bills have been enacted in state legislative environments that are broadly hostile to trans people and especially youth, on issues beyond bathroom access. In 2020 through 2023, twenty-three states passed laws prohibiting trans students from participating in sports consistent with their gender identity; this includes all of the bathroom bill states.[144] Twenty-two states, again including all of the bathroom bill states, ban at least some forms of best-practice medical care for trans youth, though some of these bans have been temporarily blocked by courts.[145] Thus, bathroom bills are but one piece of a larger effort to deny full social citizenship to trans Americans, especially trans youth, by limiting their access to health care, sports, and educational opportunities.

Finally, a few states have enacted statutes that do not quite meet the definition of bathroom bills as described above, but have various impacts on bathroom access for trans people. Tennessee, for example, enacted a statute requiring businesses and other organizations that allow individuals to use the bathroom consistent with their gender identity to post a large sign at the entrance stating in all capital letters: "THIS FACILITY MAINTAINS A POLICY OF ALLOWING THE USE OF RESTROOMS BY EITHER BIOLOGICAL SEX, REGARDLESS OF THE

---

[141] J. Gill-Peterson, *Histories of the transgender child* (Minneapolis: University of Minnesota Press, 2018), 2.

[142] Gill-Peterson, *Histories*, 61,196.   [143] Gill-Peterson, *Histories*, 196.

[144] Movement Advancement Project, "Bans on transgender youth participation in sports," 2023, accessed July 7, 2023, www.lgbtmap.org/equality-maps/sports_participation_bans.

[145] Movement Advancement Project, "Health care laws and policies," 2023, accessed August 17, 2023, www.lgbtmap.org/equality-maps/healthcare_laws_and_policies/youth_medical_care_bans.

DESIGNATION ON THE RESTROOM."[146] And, in 2023, overriding the governor's veto, Kansas passed a law defining biological sex narrowly and instructing courts to review sex-segregated bathroom policies using intermediate scrutiny and (in so many words) to find them to be constitutional.[147] Although this law does not explicitly require schools or other locations to bar trans people from bathrooms that match their gender identity, it is widely understood to have the intent of restricting trans women from accessing single-sex spaces designated for women.[148]

Trans-exclusionary bathroom policies are highly partisan. Of the eleven policies enacted across ten states, all were party unity votes, meaning a majority of Republicans voted in favor of the proposed policy and a majority of Democrats voted against it. The only quasi-exception was in the North Carolina Senate, where Democrats walked out of the chamber in protest rather than vote on the state's bathroom bill – ultimately an even stronger sign of dissent than a unanimous "no" vote from the party.[149] In eight of the twenty-four roll calls, there was no bipartisanship in terms of voting, with all Republicans voting yes and all Democrats either voting no or walking out in protest. These numbers are summarized in Table 4.

Table 4 Final passage votes on trans-exclusionary bathroom bills

States Enacting Policy, 2016–2023	10 states, 11 policies
Total Number of Final Passage Votes	21*
Percent Unanimous	0
Percent Party Unity Votes	100

***Note:** North Carolina Senate vote excluded from analysis due to Democratic walk-out.

---

[146] Tennessee Code Annotated, sec. 68-120-120. Notice of policy of allowing use of restrooms by either biological sex. In 2022, a U.S. District Court found that the statute violated the First Amendment by forcing businesses to "communicate a misleading and controversial government-mandated message that they would not otherwise display," and Tennessee has not thus far appealed the judgement. *Bongo Prods., LLC v. Lawrence*, 2022 U.S. Dist. LEXIS 88536 (2022).

[147] Kansas SB 180 (2023). The mandate for courts to utilize intermediate scrutiny also applies to other sex-segregated facilities beyond bathrooms.

[148] R. Conlon, "Will strict new anti-trans laws in Kansas keep people and companies away?" *KMUW Wichita*, May 3, 2023, www.kmuw.org/news/2023-05-03/kansas-anti-transgender-law-bathroom-bill-athletes-gender.

[149] B. Smith, "Senate Democrats walk out on vote overturning 'bathroom' ordinance," *The Carolina Journal*, March 24, 2016, www.carolinajournal.com/senate-democrats-walk-out-of-vote-overturning-bathroom-ordinance/. Because of this walkout, this vote is excluded from the party unity analysis in Table 4.

4.2 Laws on Gender Neutral Signage for Single Stall Bathrooms

In contrast to bathroom bills, some states and municipalities have taken steps to protect or expand bathroom access for trans people. These policies have taken various forms, but one common, low-cost approach is to require all single-stall bathrooms to have "gender neutral" or "all gender" signage as opposed to sex-specific signage. Although these policies do not address access to multiple-user facilities, the use of gender neutral signage can make single-user bathrooms more welcoming for trans and non-binary people. This type of policy also has positive spillovers for other groups, reducing waiting times compared to gendered restrooms by allowing a person of any gender to use the first available bathroom, and benefiting caretakers accompanying a child or disabled person into the bathroom.

Municipalities were the first to experiment with regulating gender-neutral signage. Washington, D.C. included amendments to its Human Rights Act in 2006 that mandated their use on single-stall bathrooms.[150] A decade later, California passed the first of these laws at the state level in 2016, and seven other states have since followed suit. Although most statutes deal exclusively with signage, Rhode Island's law also requires new and renovated state and municipal buildings to proactively include a gender-neutral, single-stall bathroom in addition to any multi-stall bathrooms made available.[151] Figure 4 indicates the states with gender neutral signage laws along with their dates of passage.

Advocates of gender neutral signage laws at the state and local levels include both state and national trans advocacy organizations and individuals.[152] Supporters emphasize safety, inclusion, and fairness, often in ways that echo ideas related to social citizenship and social inclusion. For example, a Bethesda county employee spoke out in favor of a county-level version of this policy in their area, making arguments based on both dignity and employment opportunities: "It is an awful feeling to know that I cannot access a bathroom during my workday without feeling fear of harassment and embarrassment."[153] In explaining her vote in favor of Vermont's statute, state representative Barbara Rachelson stated that the bill would "bring safety to people who get

---

[150] District of Columbia Municipal Regulations (2006), sec. 4-802.

[151] State of Rhode Island General Laws, sec. 23-27.3-702.

[152] S. Bohnel, "Advocates speak in favor of bill establishing gender-inclusive restrooms in county buildings, certain businesses," *Bethesda Magazine*, March 9, 2022, https://bethesdamagazine .com/bethesda-beat/government/advocates-speak-in-favor-of-bill-establishing-gender-inclusive-restrooms-in-county-buildings-certain-businesses/; T. Ring, "California adopts groundbreaking all-gender restroom access law," *The Advocate*, September 29, 2016, www.advocate.com/politics/ 2016/9/29/california-adopts-groundbreaking-all-gender-restroom-access-law.

[153] Bohnel, "Advocates speak."

Figure 4 Map of state laws requiring gender neutral signage on single stall bathrooms in the United States

threatened by picking what others deem the 'wrong bathroom.'"[154] And the sponsor of New York's bill on single-stall bathroom signage argued that it was about more than just bathrooms but about "fighting for a person's right to exist in the world free from harassment and discrimination."[155] Each of these statements speaks to social citizenship in the sense of making it safe for people to access public spaces and workplaces on an equal basis.

In the eight states where gender neutral signage has become law, it has tended to pass by wide margins, gaining the support of around 83 percent of state senators and 87 percent of state house/assembly members in these states. Support for gender neutral signage laws has also typically been bipartisan, with at least one member of both parties supporting the legislation in almost every chamber where it passed. The only exception is Maine, where the provision was part of a broader human rights law that, among other things, added anti-discrimination protections based on gender identity.[156]

Although signage laws have tended to gain bipartisan support, overall support was substantially stronger among Democrats, with zero Democrats voting against this policy across eight state legislatures. Of the sixteen final passage votes in the data, half were party unity votes in which a majority of Democrats voted in favor of the policy and a majority of Republicans opposed the policy. These numbers are summarized in Table 5.

In many states, however, signage on single-stall bathrooms will be moving out of the hands of politicians with the ongoing adoption of the

---

[154] Journal of the House (Vermont), 772 (2017).   [155] New York SB 6479A (2019).
[156] Maine HP 1216 (2019).

Table 5 Final passage votes/floor decisions on gender
neutral signage policy

States Enacting Policy, 2016–2021	8
Total Number of Final Floor Decisions	16
Percent Unanimous	31
Percent Party Unity Votes	50

2021 International Plumbing Code (IPC). Thirty-seven states use this code as the basis of their state's plumbing code, and the 2021 version includes a requirement that single-stall bathrooms be labelled in a way that indicates they are accessible to everyone regardless of gender.[157] Advocates for these changes to the IPC included the National Center for Transgender Equality as well as Stalled!, a group that works around inclusive bathroom design.[158]

Although states and localities can modify or adapt the code to their specific needs, the inclusion of this policy within a broader code covering a number of technical rules related to plumbing means that many states and cities can adopt a gender neutral signage policy without an issue-specific up-or-down vote and without the need for a sponsor to advocate specifically on this issue. Although states adopt and roll out current versions of the IPC over the course of several years – generally, states used the 2018 IPC or earlier as of the 2023 legislative session – over time, adoption of the 2021 code will likely lead to many more states requiring gender neutral signage.[159] The IPC's main alternative, the Uniform Plumbing Code (UPC), also includes a similar provision about gender neutral signage in single stall bathrooms in its 2021 code.[160]

Finally, an extension of gender-neutral signage on single stall bathrooms is multi-stall gender-neutral or all gender bathrooms. These multi-stall bathrooms typically differ from standard multi-stall bathrooms found in the United States in that each toilet has a floor-to-ceiling door to increase privacy, and

---

[157] "International Plumbing Code changes facilitate all-gender restrooms," *The Architect's Newspaper*, March 27, 2019, www.archpaper.com/2019/03/international-plumbing-code-changes-facilitate-all-gender-restrooms/. Note that states lag behind the year of code release in adopting new versions of the IPC. For more information, see: International Code Council, "International Plumbing Code (IPC)," International Code Council, 2023, accessed February 13, 2023, www.iccsafe.org/content/international-plumbing-code-ipc-home-page/.

[158] "International Plumbing Code changes facilitate all-gender restrooms."

[159] International Code Council, "International Plumbing Code (IPC)."

[160] 2021 Uniform Plumbing Code 422.2.1: Single Use Toilet Facilities.

then all users share a common bank of sinks. In most parts of the country, this style of bathroom requires a code variance, although this is starting to change in some municipalities and states.[161] Both California and Illinois have passed laws that allow municipalities to include all gender multi-stall bathrooms as a standard option in their building codes.[162]

4.3 Anti-Discrimination Laws Addressing Multi-Stall Bathrooms

Several states have enacted anti-discrimination measures that include gender identity and apply to either public accommodations, public schools, or both.[163] But, while some state and federal courts have found that anti-discrimination laws that prohibit discrimination on the basis of sex or gender identity require allowing a transgender person to use the bathroom that conforms with their gender identity, the Supreme Court has specifically declined to rule on this issue. Federal regulatory guidance on this topic has changed with each of the past three presidential administrations and has been challenged in court, leading to uncertainty at the national level.[164] Because the applicability of anti-discrimination law to multi-stall bathrooms is unclear at the federal level, some states and municipal governments have enacted anti-discrimination ordinances and statutes that specifically address the issue of bathroom access for trans people generally or for trans students in public school settings. Two states' laws are of particular note.

In 2013, California amended its School Code to elaborate on existing anti-discrimination protections for students. While state law already included gender identity as a protected characteristic, the new law clarified that trans and gender non-conforming students must be allowed to participate in sports and utilize sex-segregated school facilities, including restrooms, in accordance with their

[161] "Design Approaches presents the pros and cons of the three most common solutions to all-gender restrooms: The single, multi-unit, and low-budget retrofit solution," 2023, accessed July 7, 2023, www.stalled.online/approaches.

[162] Cal. Health & Saf. Code § 118507 (2022) and Illinois Public Act 103-0518 (2023).

[163] Movement Advancement Project, "Safe schools laws," 2023, accessed July 7, 2023, www.lgbtmap.org/equality-maps/safe_school_laws/discrimination; Movement Advancement Project, "Nondiscrimination laws," 2023, accessed July 7, 2023, www.lgbtmap.org/equality-maps/non_discrimination_laws/public-accommodations.

[164] J. W. Peters, J. Becker, and J. H. Davis, "Trump rescinds rules on bathrooms for transgender students," *The New York Times*, February 22, 2017, www.nytimes.com/2017/02/22/us/politics/devos-sessions-transgender-students-rights.html; E. L. Green, "New Biden rules would bar discrimination against transgender students," *The New York Times*, June 23, 2022, www.nytimes.com/2022/06/23/us/politics/biden-transgender-students-discrimination.html; R. Iafolla and J. E. Moreno, "Federal judge topples EEOC's LGBT bathroom, pronoun guidance," *Bloomberg Law*, October 3, 2022, https://news.bloomberglaw.com/daily-labor-report/federal-judge-topples-eeocs-lgbt-bathroom-and-pronoun-guidance.

gender identity.[165] The Senate vote was a strict party line vote, and the Assembly vote was a party unity vote with some Democrats opposing the bill.

Both the California Assembly and Senate produced legislative analyses of the bill. These analyses contained significant overlap, and so are considered together. The analyses emphasize the harms of exclusion to trans students who are not able to access appropriate facilities, including both physical consequences like dehydration and academic consequences such as missed class. The analyses also a school climate survey indicating that LGBT students were more likely to feel unsafe in school and to miss school for this reason. They quote an amicus brief from a related court case filed by three LGBT rights organizations, which made an explicit comparison to the racial segregation of bathrooms: "claims of discomfort in the presence of a minority group propped up decades of racial segregation in housing, education, and access to public facilities like restrooms and drinking fountains."[166]

Interest groups supporting the bill included multiple types of organizations, including those focused on LGBT rights and civil rights more generally as well as labor groups, groups representing teachers and parents, and some school districts. Three groups took the lead, specifically Equality California, the Gay-Straight Alliance Network, and the Transgender Law Center. Opponents included religious and conservative organizations, including the California Catholic Conference and the Traditional Values Coalition.[167]

Massachusetts took a different approach to an inclusive bathroom law, focusing on public accommodations as opposed to only public schools in a 2016 statute. The law requires any public accommodation that is legally segregated on the basis of sex to allow access consistent with gender identity.[168] Several unsuccessful amendments to the bill were proposed during the legislative process. These included exemptions for bathrooms, locker rooms, and showering facilities; requirements that trans people provide documentation of medical or legal transition; and civil or criminal penalties for "improper" assertion of gender

---

[165] California AB 1266 (2013). Information on bill text, votes, and legislative analyses can all be found through the California Legislative Information service, available at: California Legislative Information, "AB-1266 pupil rights: Sex-segregated school programs and activities," 2013, accessed March 1, 2023, https://leginfo.legislature.ca.gov/faces/billTextClient.xhtml?bill_id=201320140AB1266.

[166] California AB 1266 (2013). Information on bill text, votes, and legislative analyses can all be found through the California Legislative Information service.

[167] California AB 1266 (2013). Information on bill text, votes, and legislative analyses can all be found through the California Legislative Information service.

[168] Massachusetts S 735 (2016). Information on bill text, votes, and amendments can all be found through the General Court of the Commonwealth of Massachusetts, available at: The General Court of the Commonwealth of Massachusetts, "An act relative to transgender anti-discrimination," 2016, https://malegislature.gov/Bills/189/S735.

identity. One even suggested that public accommodations could designate one bathroom as "transgendered" [sic] and then deny trans people access to other facilities. Ultimately, each of these amendments were either rejected or with-drawn. The bill passed the House with a party unity vote and the Senate with a voice vote.

Following the adoption of the Massachusetts law, there was a statewide referendum that attempted to repeal the law through a ballot measure. The campaign against the measure focused largely on women's safety and risks of sexual assault – although it is important to note that research indicates no increased risk for cis women after the implementation of trans-inclusive bath-room policies.[169] A coalition called Freedom for All Massachusetts supported the anti-discrimination law, and included broad support from business, labor, education, and sports groups; law enforcement; religious leaders; and state elected officials.[170] Ultimately, Massachusetts voters approved of the original law by a wide margin of 68 percent to 32 percent; voters not only approved of the law statewide, but in every county.[171]

While California and Massachusetts are the only two states to address bathroom access specifically in state law, other states have tackled this issue through regulatory guidance or rulemaking processes. Twenty-two states include gender identity in state civil rights or anti-discrimination laws that cover public accommodations, and seventeen states include gender identity in corresponding legislation that applies to public schools. Of these, fourteen include administrative guidance through the state Board of Education that requires or at least recommends inclusive bathroom policies for trans public school students. Eight include similar provisions for public accommodations through state civil rights commissions or similar bodies.[172] A summary of these policies is found in Table 6.

---

[169] K. Weintraub, "Massachusetts law on transgender protections draws strong support ahead of vote," *Washington Post*, October 30, 2018, www.washingtonpost.com/national/massachusetts-law-on-transgender-protections-draws-strong-support-ahead-of-vote/2018/10/30/7c116c4c-dbe4-11e8-85df-7a6b4d25cfbb_story.html. See also: A. Hasenbush, A. R. Flores, and J. L. Herman, "Gender identity nondiscrimination laws in public accommodations: A review of evidence regarding safety and privacy in public restrooms, locker rooms, and changing rooms," *Sexuality Research and Social Policy* 16, no. 1 (2019): 70–83.

[170] "About Freedom for All Massachusetts," 2018, accessed March 2, 2023, https://web.archive.org/web/20180528214716/https://www.freedommassachusetts.org/about/.

[171] "2018 – Statewide – Question 3," Secretary of the Commonwealth of Massachusetts, 2018, accessed March 2, 2023, https://electionstats.state.ma.us/ballot_questions/view/7305/.

[172] This information was compiled by starting with a list of state policies on gender identity discrimination from the Movement Advancement Project and then crosschecking with state agency websites and news coverage to identify bathroom-specific policies and guidance. See Movement Advancement Project, "Nondiscrimination laws"; Movement Advancement Project, "Safe schools laws."

Table 6 State statutes and administrative polices on gender identity anti-discrimination and bathroom access, 2022

Statute or policy	Number of states, 2022	List of states
Bathroom-specific anti-discrimination statute	2	CA, MA
Gender identity anti-discrimination statute applying to schools, public accommodations, or both (may not include reference to bathrooms)	22	CA, CO, CT, DE, HI, IA, IL, KS, MA, MD, ME, MN, NH, NJ, NM, NV, NY, OR, RI, VA, VT, WA
Bathroom-specific Board of Education guidance (applying to public schools)	14	CA, CO, CT, HI, IL, MA, ME, MI, MN, NJ, NY, OR, RI, WA
Bathroom-specific Civil Rights Commission guidance (applying to public accommodations)	8	CA, CO, HI, IA, IL, MA, NJ, NY

Of course, regulatory guidance is easier to overturn than statute. One particularly relevant example is Virginia. A 2020 Virginia law requires schools to adopt policies concerning trans students that align with "evidence-based best practices," including with regard to access to sex-segregated school facilities.[173] The next year, in 2021, a Virginia school district settled a high profile, years-spanning court case over limiting bathroom access for a trans student for over a million dollars.[174] And, the Virginia Human Rights Act includes protection for gender identity in both education and public accommodations.[175]

Despite this context, Republican Governor Glenn Youngkin directed the Board of Education to issue new regulatory guidance, requiring all school districts to adopt policies restricting bathroom use by sex assigned at birth, among other policies targeting trans youth. This would have been a sharp reversal from BOE policy under the previous Democratic governor, under which schools were supposed to grant students access to sex-segregated facilities in accordance with their gender identity.[176] Unsurprisingly given the prior legal context in the state, Youngkin's move was met with strong opposition. The final model policy adopted by the state, after threats of lawsuits, is ultimately ambiguous with respect to trans students' rights to access facilities, stating that "[s]tudents shall use bathrooms that correspond to his or her sex, except to the extent that federal law otherwise requires" – and then citing a federal court decision that affirmed the right of a trans student to access facilities consistent with his gender identity, without further clarification.[177] Thus, it is unclear how districts will interpret this policy, if they adopt it at all.[178]

Virginia's experience illustrates just how unstable bathroom policies in the states are in the current political climate. State laws and policies on bathroom access consistent with gender identity run the full spectrum from inclusive policies that legally guarantee access for trans and gender non-conforming

---

[173] Code of Virginia, sec. 22.1-23.3.   [174] Natanson, "Virginia school board."

[175] Code of Virginia, sec. 2.2-3900-22.3902.

[176] H. Natanson, "Virginia policy latest attempt to restrict rights of transgender students," *Washington Post*, September 17, 2022, www.washingtonpost.com/education/2022/09/16/trans-students-virginia-bathroom-sports/.

[177] K. Elwood, "Va. killed bills aimed at trans youths. Here's where the debate moves next," *Washington Post*, March 1, 2023, www.washingtonpost.com/education/2023/03/01/virginia-education-transgender-youth/. Virginia Department of Education, "Model policies on ensuring privacy, dignity, and respect for all students and parents in Virginia's public schools," 2023, accessed January 3, 2024, www.doe.virginia.gov/programs-services/student-services/student-assistance-programming/gender-diversity; N. Cline, "Virginia rules commission objects to proposed transgender policies," *Virginia Mercury*, December 19, 2022, www.virginiamercury.com/2022/12/19/virginia-rules-commission-objects-to-proposed-transgender-policies/.

[178] K. Elwood, "What to know about Virginia's transgender student model policies," *Washington Post*, August 18, 2023, www.washingtonpost.com/education/2023/07/23/virginia-transgender-model-policies-faq/.

people to policies that limit access based on sex assigned at birth, especially for K-12 students. The ability of trans and gender non-conforming students to access educational opportunities thus varies dramatically from state-to-state, school district-to-school district, and year-to-year. Especially when it comes to regulatory guidance, these policies can seesaw from election to election.

5 Bathrooms and Disability Accessibility

Sex-segregated bathrooms, along with all their complications for trans and gender non-conforming communities, also present barriers to disabled people, some of whom need a caregiver of a different gender to accompany them into a bathroom. Of course, disabled people encounter many other structural and architectural barriers when seeking to use a bathroom outside the home. Phillipa Wiseman, for example, writes about how toilet design and access is crucial for understanding "how our bodies are perceived, and our citizenship imagined" – and for disabled people, both the message and physical reality is often one of "nonbelonging."[179]

Unlike the previous sections that focus primarily on state-level policies, this section begins with a brief overview of the impact of the Americans with Disabilities Act (ADA) on bathroom accessibility, as well as the limitations of this law for disability accessibility. I then analyze two state-level policies that aim to go beyond the ADA in different ways. Ally's Law or the Restroom Access Act (RAA) aims to extend accessibility for individuals with Crohn's, colitis, and related medical conditions. The second policy, which has been less widely adopted, requires some public locations to provide changing tables for adults with disabilities who require access to a space for diapering and caretaker assistance. In both of these policy areas, I outline the landscape of state-level policies, analyze the impact of both partisanship and interest groups, and draw connections to social citizenship.

5.1 The Americans with Disabilities Act and Access to Public Accommodations

Congress began to set federal standards for disability accessibility in buildings with the Architectural Barriers Act in 1968. This law applied only to federally funded buildings and lacked any enforcement mechanism.[180] During this same decade, toilet design began to become more inclusive with innovations such as

---

[179] P. Wiseman, "Lifting the lid: Disabled toilets as sites of belonging and embodied citizenship," *The Sociological Review* 67, no. 4 (2019): 788–789.

[180] M. F. Raffa, "Removing architectural barriers: The Architectural Barriers Act of 1968," *Mental and Physical Disability Law Reporter* 9, no. 4 (1985): 304–308.

grab bars and more accessible sinks – first as optional modifications in private homes, but with more widespread installation in public spaces starting in 1980.[181]

Rights to equal access to all public accommodations for disabled people was extended by the Americans with Disabilities Act (ADA) in 1990, though it is important to note that the law's guarantees do have limitations. The ADA was signed into law by Republican President George H. W. Bush, as the result of bipartisan efforts to move the legislation through Congress.[182] Unlike other civil rights legislation, supporters and lobbyists intentionally avoided public attention and media coverage prior to the law's passage, in an effort to avoid opposition and backlash.[183]

Of course, the ADA encompasses much more than just accessible bathrooms and, indeed, more than accessible buildings and facilities more generally. Timothy Cook writes that "the primary evil addressed in the ADA was the segregation that continues to impose an isolated, denigrated existence upon persons with disabilities."[184] The law aimed to end a legacy of segregation created and maintained not only by private actors but also legislatures and courts, and this could be accomplished only partly through changes in the design of public spaces. Still, the physical characteristics of those spaces is important for social citizenship. Robert Bergdorf explains:

> Architectural barriers are another significant obstacle to the full participation of Americans with disabilities in mainstream society. The presence of physical barriers not only effectively bars people with certain disabilities from visiting social, commercial, and recreational establishments, but also enhances the population with disabilities' perception that they are unwelcome.[185]

Thus removing architectural barriers both opens up public spaces to be accessed by disabled people and sends a message that they are full members of the community. This dual nature of social citizenship as it relates to bathroom access is echoed in David Serlin's account of a major protest by disability rights

---

[181] D. Serlin, "Pissing without pity: Disability, gender, and the public toilet," in *Toilet: Public restrooms and the politics of sharing*, ed. H. Molotch and L. Noren (New York: New York University Press, 2010), 171.

[182] L. J. Davis, *Enabling acts: The hidden story of how the Americans with Disabilities Act gave the largest US minority its rights* (Boston: Beacon Press, 2015). The original ADA was enacted in 1990, with significant amendments (also passed with broad bipartisan support) being enacted in 2008.

[183] Davis, *Enabling acts*, 229; M. Johnson, "Before its time: Public perception of disability rights, the Americans with Disabilities Act, and the future of access and accommodation disabilities," *Washington University Journal of Law & Policy* 23 (2007): 121.

[184] T. M. Cook, "The Americans with Disabilities Act: The move to integration," *Temple Law Review* 64, no. 2 (1991): 398.

[185] R. L. Burgdorf Jr., "Equal members of the community: The public accommodations provisions of the Americans with Disabilities Act," *Temple Law Review* 64, no. 2 (1991): 554.

activists in 1977, in which protesters occupied the San Francisco office of the Department of Health, Education, and Welfare for twenty-five days, despite the lack of adequate and accessible toilet facilities. Serlin writes that for some activists, doing so risked their health and even their lives, but this was part of their message, because "their inability to use the toilet was both symbolic of and material evidence for their exclusion from the public sphere."[186]

Accessible bathrooms were emphasized by disability rights activists in congressional hearings for the ADA, in large part "because it is impractical to travel outside the home if one does not have access to restrooms."[187] Thus without the construction of accessible restrooms, people who use wheelchairs or otherwise need an accessible toilet are unable to fully engage in the public sphere. The text of the ADA addresses accessible bathrooms most specifically in the context of public transportation, especially by rail.[188] Title III of the Act, which is the section dealing with public accommodations, does not explicitly reference bathrooms but more generally guarantees that "[no] individual shall be discriminated against on the basis of disability in the full and equal enjoyment of the goods, services, facilities, privileges, advantages, or accommodations of any place of public accommodation ... "[189] With regard to accessible bathrooms specifically, these fall under the requirement that new and renovated facilities be "readily accessible to and usable by individuals with disabilities," which is then translated into specific architectural requirements through the federal regulatory process.[190] For example, the 2010 ADA Standards for Accessible Design have specific requirements for restrooms related to turning space for a wheelchair, the size of water closets (toilet stalls), the height of toilet seats in accessible stalls, and so on.[191]

All that said, despite the real progress made by the ADA, the law has serious shortcomings. Foremost among them are provisions in the law that allow public accommodations to exclude disabled people and avoid making their facilities accessible when doing so is not "readily achievable" or is "structurally impracticable." When undertaking renovations, public accommodations must consider accessibility but may balance it with cost.[192] As Mary Johnson puts it, the ADA is "a civil rights bill with an economic loophole built in."[193] In the absence of a strong federal enforcement mechanism, disabled individuals must rely on

---

[186] Serlin, "Pissing without pity."   [187] Colker, "Public restrooms," 147.
[188] The Americans with Disabilities Act of 1990, Public Law 101-336, 104 Stat. 327, Title II, Subtitle B, Part II.
[189] The Americans with Disabilities Act of 1990, Title III, sec. 302(a).
[190] The Americans with Disabilities Act of 1990, Title III, sec. 303.
[191] Department of Justice, 2010 ADA Standards for Accessible Design, Chapter 6.
[192] The Americans with Disabilities Act of 1990, Title II, sec. 301 and 303.
[193] Johnson, "Before its time," 123.

lawsuits – often at substantial personal burden – to enforce the ADA.[194] Even the litigation model of enforcement faces additional hurdles, as the ADA carves out numerous exceptions and allowable defenses for defendants that are not present in other civil rights legislation.[195]

Because the ADA does not fully accomplish the goal of comprehensive accessibility in public spaces, some states have enacted legislation that aims to increase access in various ways, including access to bathroom facilities. Although these state policies also fall short of full accessibility, they do add new protections for people who have specific challenges accessing bathrooms. In addition to providing greater physical access to public spaces, each of these state statutes also sends important messages about dignity and belonging.

5.2 Ally's Law or Restroom Access Acts

Ally's Law, also known as the Restroom Access Act (RAA) or the Crohn's and Colitis Fairness Act, is probably the most wide-spread disability-related bathroom access law outside of the ADA, and it aims to increase access for individuals with an urgent medical need for a bathroom when out in public. Maryland enacted the first version of this law in 1987, but the policy gained publicity and momentum after the activism of teenager Ally Bain, who advocated for its passage in Illinois in 2005.[196] As of 2023, twenty states had enacted some form of this policy.

State-level RAAs require certain retail establishments to allow customers with specific medical conditions to use an employee bathroom when another public bathroom is not available. These conditions typically include Crohn's disease, colitis, irritable bowel disease or irritable bowel syndrome, and use of an ostomy device. Michigan also explicitly includes pregnancy as a covered condition.[197]

Although the basic idea behind the RAA is consistent across states, there is considerable variation in terms of the details. Most states provide some liability protection for businesses allowing access under the act, include exceptions for employee bathrooms in locations that might endanger the safety of customers or impact the security of the business, and do not require businesses to change the physical setup of their employee bathrooms or meet the legal standards for public restrooms. Ohio merely "encourages" businesses to allow access to bathrooms for those with eligible medical conditions, while other states require

---

[194] Johnson, "Before its time," 124.

[195] A. Kanter, "The Americans with Disabilities Act at 25 years: Lessons to learn from the convention on the rights of people with disabilities," *Drake Law Review* 63, no. 3 (2015): 832.

[196] S. Wilson, "State-level activism in the disability context: Ensuring protections for people with disabilities through American federalism and the Fourteenth Amendment equal protection clause," *Journal of Health & Biomedical Law* 15, no. 2 (2019): 204.

[197] Michigan Compiled Laws, sec. 446.72.

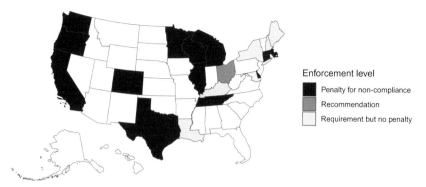

Figure 5 Map of Restroom Access Acts by enforcement mechanism

access but don't specify a penalty for non-compliance. Ten states provide for monetary fines of between $50 and $200 for establishments that do not comply. Figure 5 provides a sense of the geographic spread of RAAs and the type of enforcement mechanism, if any.

State policies also vary in what is required of disabled customers. While all define specific medical conditions that customers must have in order to obtain access to employee restrooms, almost all states (sixteen in total) also require customers to "prove" their medical condition in some way, such as a doctor's note or medical identification card. Three states provide a specific punishment for forged or fraudulent use of medical evidence – Michigan and Washington with a misdemeanor, and Wisconsin with up to a $200 fine.

As mentioned above, Ally Bain was a major force behind the passage of the RAA in Illinois in 2005, and she remains a public face of this issue. Although it was not the first in the nation, Illinois's law has become a model for other states in part through Bain's efforts. Bain has Crohn's disease, and at the age of fourteen was denied access to an employee restroom. Bain publicly defecated herself as a result, and then began to advocate around the issue of restroom access in her state.[198] She worked with her state representative, Representative Kathy Ryg, who she had recently met on a school field trip, and she ultimately testified before the state legislature.[199] Ryg also cited the involvement of three interest groups in helping to advocate for and shape the Illinois law that she ultimately introduced: the Crohn's and Colitis Foundation of America, the Gastro-Intestinal Research Foundation, and the Illinois Retail Merchants Association.[200]

---

[198] Wilson, "State-level activism," 184.

[199] S. Owens, "The grassroots movement to change the nation's public restroom laws," *US News & World Report*, December 20, 2012, www.usnews.com/news/articles/2012/12/20/the-grass roots-movement-to-change-the-nations-public-restroom-laws.

[200] L. Aukett, "One voice makes a difference," *Ostomy Quarterly* 43, no. 1 (2005): 67.

The Crohn's and Colitis Foundation (CCF) in particular has advocated for the passage of the RAA across the country since 2005. It offers a model bill to states interested in enacting this type of policy. Notably, the CCF's model bill is more expansive than the legislation that has actually been passed: it does not require proof from customers of their medical condition and would levy a much larger fine – a minimum of $1000 – on businesses who violate the law, more than any state currently does.[201] Although the CCF does not recommend that states require evidence of a medical condition, it does provide members with identification cards that they can use in retail establishments, which are specifically mentioned in some state legislation as an acceptable form of evidence.[202]

Opposition to RAAs has come primarily from retail businesses and gas stations, largely related to concerns around shoplifting, security, and liability.[203] Some states have responded to these types of concerns explicitly in the drafting of RAAs. And, in practice, there have not been significant problems or complaints from businesses in states that have enacted RAAs.[204] Another concern about RAAs from those who advocate for greater restroom access is that it carves out special access for individuals with specific, diagnosed medical conditions as opposed to expanding access for everyone. Thus, this law can help advance a norm among business owners that they can ignore customer needs for bathroom access if individuals don't have a diagnosed condition or don't physically have proof of their condition with them.[205]

Advocates for RAAs, on the other hand, have argued that individuals with Crohn's and similar diseases suffer ongoing humiliation and anxiety around bathroom access, and do need special protection under the law in order to feel comfortable in public spaces.[206] At the same time, the impact of RAAs may be more symbolic than practical. Richard Weinmeyer conducted interviews with individuals with inflammatory bowel disease and found that many felt unable to take advantage of the policy due to lack of knowledge among store employees and the requirement to reveal personal medical information in order to access employee restrooms.[207]

[201] Crohn's and Colitis Foundation, "Restroom Access Act (model legislation)," 2019, accessed June 28, 2022, www.crohnscolitisfoundation.org/sites/default/files/2019-10/Restroom%20Access%20model%20legislation.docx.pdf.

[202] "Restroom access," Crohn's and Colitis Foundation, 2022, accessed June 28, 2022, www.crohnscolitisfoundation.org/get-involved/be-an-advocate/restroom-access.

[203] Owens, "Grassroots."

[204] A. J. Tresca, "How the Restroom Access Act helps those with IBD," *Very Well Health*, May 2, 2020.

[205] Banks, "Disappearing public toilet," 1086–1087.

[206] Owens, "Grassroots."; A. Cimo, AB 283 Alex Cimo testimony (Nevada: Nevada State Assembly, Committee of Health and Human Services, 2021).

[207] Weinmeyer, "Lavatories," 429.

Table 7 Final passage votes/floor decisions on the
Restroom Access Act

States Enacting Policy, 2005–2022	19
Number of Final Floor Decisions	38
Percent Unanimous	55
Percent Party Unity Votes	8

Support for RAAs has generally been bipartisan, with about half the recorded final votes in the 2000s–2020s being unanimous – some unanimous roll calls and others passed through unanimous consent or similar procedures.[208] In contrast, party unity votes that pit the majority of one party against the majority of the other party were less common in the passage of RAAs. One of only three party unity votes on this policy came on a bill that included an RAA provision in a larger bill that addressed issues relating to health care and anti-discrimination. These results are summarized in Table 7.

5.3 Universal Changing Table Legislation

Less widespread than the RAA is another state policy that aims to increase bathroom access for disabled people: requirements for certain types of buildings to include changing tables for adults within universal changing spaces or family restrooms. While it is relatively common to see changing tables for babies, larger facilities that can be used by disabled teenagers and adults and their caretakers are both more expensive and less available to those who need them. But, without access to universal changing tables, older children and adults who use diapers and require assistance from a caretaker may be stuck at home – excluded from public spaces entirely – or forced to use unsanitary bathroom floors for changing purposes, with implications for both health and dignity.[209] Five states have enacted statutes addressing this issue as indicated in Figure 6.

Adult changing facilities typically include an enclosed room that is large enough for both a person using a power wheelchair and a caretaker. The changing tables themselves are adjustable height and sturdy enough to accommodate an adult. Exact requirements vary by state but may also include rules around the

---

[208] Maryland's 1987 statute is excluded from the analysis.

[209] J. Call, "A mom's mission: Bill seeks to require adult changing tables in Florida public restrooms," *Tallahasee Democrat*, December 25, 2019, www.tallahassee.com/story/news/polit ics/2019/12/09/bill-seeks-require-adult-changing-tables-florida-public-restrooms/ 4354123002/.

Figure 6 Map of universal changing table legislation in the states

inclusion of things like sinks, soap dispensers, etc.[210] California's 2015 bill requires the installation of adult changing table facilities in new construction and major renovations in "commercial place[s] of public amusement [such as] an auditorium, convention center, cultural complex, exhibition hall, permanent amusement park, sports arena, or theater or movie house." It only applies to facilities with a capacity of 2,500 or more individuals, and specifically excludes higher education buildings and agricultural associations.[211] Arizona's 2019 law and Maryland's 2021 law apply only to public entities such as state and local governments and agencies.[212] New Hampshire's 2019 law is the most expansive in terms of the locations it covers, requiring universal changing stations in any new construction of public accommodations serving more than 1,500 people per day.[213] Minnesota's 2023 statute is vague, requiring that adult-size changing tables be included as a requirement in the state building code, but leaving the specifics of implementation up to the commissioner of labor and industry.[214]

Advocacy around universal changing table legislation has varied but often comes from the mothers of disabled children and adults, sometimes working through individual and local efforts and sometimes through larger organizations like the Changing Spaces Campaign.[215] In California, the first state to pass universal changing table legislation, the effort was spearheaded by Alisa Rosillo,

---

[210] See, for example, New Hampshire Revised Statutes, Title XII, sec. 155.80.

[211] California Health and Safety Code, sec. 19952.5.

[212] Arizona Revised Statutes, sec. 41-1444. Maryland Code, State Finance and Procurement, sec. 2-801-2-803.

[213] New Hampshire Revised Statutes, Title XII, sec. 155.80.

[214] Minnesota Statutes (2023), 326B.106 General Powers of Commissioner of Labor and Industry

[215] Call, "Mom's mission."; *A bathroom's standard changing table doesn't fit families with special needs*, aired May 28, 2021, on 9News. www.9news.com/video/news/local/next/bathrooms-chan ging-table-families-special-needs/73-9d380ca3-cc1d-40af-8d3c-09ea893f748e; "Changing Spaces campaign," 2023, accessed November 15, 2023, www.changingspacescampaign.com/.

a disability advocate and mother of two disabled teenagers who required assistance with diapering. Rosillo worked on multiple pieces of legislation in California related to disability rights, including expanding bathroom access.[216]

Minnesota's recent legislation was spearheaded by Sarah St. Louis, the mother of a child with traumatic brain injury, and Linda Hood, who uses a wheelchair and was Miss Wheelchair Minnesota in 2022. In discussing the importance of the bill, St. Louis discussed both public health and dignity concerns around the lack of appropriate spaces to change her son's diapers, describing the experience of changing him on a bathroom floor as "really undignified, it's not sanitary, it's not safe and it's humiliating."[217] Advocacy efforts include legislative work but also working with businesses, churches, and government buildings to voluntarily install adult changing stations.[218]

Opposition to installing universal changing stations often focuses on the costs to government – and in states where private entities must comply with new regulations – to business. In Maryland, for example, the Maryland Association of Counties was the sole opposing witness during legislative hearings, arguing that universal changing station legislation would increase both construction and enforcement costs for county governments. In contrast, organizations testifying in favor of the legislation made arguments focused on dignity and inclusion. For example, AARP Maryland called the absence of universal changing tables "isolating and degrading" and the Maryland Catholic Conference called the legislation "life-affirming." The Maryland Developmental Disabilities Council's testimony explicitly connects to core ideas of social citizenship, arguing that the statute would provide more work opportunities for disabled people, as well as allowing them to "be fully integrated ... [and] meaningfully participate in their communities."[219]

The level of bipartisanship in final call roll calls for adult changing table legislation has varied widely by the state in which the policy was enacted. California's law was highly partisan, with both chambers seeing party

---

[216] "Concord mom receives advocacy award, state assembly recognition for work on successful adult changing table bill," *Family Voices of California*, June 28, 2016, www.familyvoicesofca .org/adult-changing-tables-federal-autism-panel-bleeding-disorders/.

[217] S. Littlefield, "Adult changing tables are now Minnesota law in all new public restrooms," *WCCO News*, May 30, 2023, www.cbsnews.com/minnesota/news/adult-changing-tables-are-now-minnesota-law-in-all-new-public-restrooms/.

[218] For an example of state-level advocacy in Ohio of this type, see "Changing Spaces campaign – Ohio chapter," 2023, accessed November 15, 2023, www.changingspacescampaign.com/ohio. See also D. King, "ODOT adding adult-sized changing tables in 28 highway rest areas by 2026," *Columbus Dispatch*, May 13, 2023, www.dispatch.com/story/news/healthcare/2023/05/18/ odot-adding-adult-sized-changing-tables-in-28-highway-rest-areas-universal-disability/ 70205223007/.

[219] Maryland General Assembly, "Health and Government Operations – witness list," 2021, accessed November 29, 2023, https://mgaleg.maryland.gov/mgawebsite/Legislation/ WitnessSignup/HB0321?ys=2021RS.

Table 8 Final passage votes/floor decisions on adult
changing table legislation

States Enacting Policy, 2015–2023	5
Number of Final Floor Decisions	10
Percent Unanimous	30
Percent Party Unity Votes	50

unity votes on final passage roll calls and few members crossing the aisle
in these votes. In this case, Democrats almost all supported the adult
changing table provision and almost all Republicans voted against it. The
same pattern appeared in Minnesota, but there the adult changing table
provision was part of a much larger budget bill. In New Hampshire, the
chambers were divided in terms of bipartisanship, with the Senate passing
the bill via voice vote, although the *New Hampshire Union Leader*
reported on the bill as being primarily supported by Democrats throughout
the legislative process.[220] In contrast, support for adult changing table
policy was much more bipartisan in Arizona and Maryland, with majorities
of both parties in both chambers in those states voting in favor of the law.
These numbers are summarized in Table 8.

As in the case of gender neutral signage for single-stall bathrooms, adult
changing stations are also beginning to be incorporated into model codes,
in this case through building codes. The International Building Code (IBC)
is even more widely used than the International Plumbing Code.[221] The
2024 version of the IBC includes a provision that will require adult
changing stations in some large facilities that serve the public and have
large occupancies, such as large movie theaters, stadiums, airports, major
highway rest stops, and educational buildings.[222] As discussed in Section
4.2, code adoption is slow and it is not guaranteed that all states and cities
using the IBC will adopt this specific provision, but the inclusion of adult
changing tables in the IBC should make adoption more widespread in the
coming years.

---

[220] D. Solomon, "NH House Democrats pass bills restricting use of plastic bags, straws," *New
Hampshire Union Leader (Manchester, NH)*, March 19, 2019, https://infoweb.newsbank.com/
apps/news/document-view?p=WORLDNEWS&docref=news/1731CFF78A5C9A68,
NewsBank.

[221] "International Code Council: Code adoptions," 2023, accessed November 28, 2023, www
.iccsafe.org/advocacy/#code-adoption-database.

[222] 2024 International Building Code, 1110.4 Adult Changing Stations, https://codes.iccsafe.org/
content/IBC2024P1/chapter-11-accessibility#IBC2024P1_Ch11_Sec1110.4

6 Conclusion: Bathrooms, Class, and Citizenship

Thus far, I have used the concept of social citizenship to explain how central bathrooms are to a right to engage in society and "belong" in public spaces. This understanding of social citizenship has two components: a more psychological message of inclusion and dignity, as well as a physical time limit – at the end of which those without access to a bathroom must either exit public spaces or risk criminalization by urinating and defecating publicly. Although in some cases only one of these elements is present in bathroom-access legislation, often these two elements are intertwined.

As noted at the beginning of this Element, academics and practitioners have often used the idea of social citizenship to analyze economic inclusion, poverty, and welfare state policies. My analysis of bathrooms and social citizenship demonstrates that, in important ways, class politics and "identity" politics are inseparable. As we have seen, the absence of accessible and adequate bathrooms can translate into a loss of both educational and employment opportunities for women and girls, for trans and gender non-conforming people, and for disabled people.

Similarly, when considering more explicitly class-based bathroom access policy issues, identity does not disappear from the picture. In the conclusion of this Element, I circle back to the economic aspect of social citizenship, with an emphasis on the ways that bathroom access intersects with employment and housing. This discussion touches on both workplace regulations and the impact of public toilet provision (or lack of provision) on people experiencing homelessness. I then expand the scope in two ways, exploring the global context of toilets and sanitation, and finally considering connections between democracy and attacks on bathroom access.

6.1 Bathrooms in the Workplace

In the 1880s, as women began to enter the workforce, states began to enact gender-specific rest or meal break policies applying only to women workers. By the mid-1900s, a majority of states had enacted these gender-specific break policies, part of larger trend of "protective legislation." But, with the enactment of Title VII prohibiting gender discrimination in employment, many of these gender-specific policies were eliminated. And, efforts to enact gender-neutral policies covering all workers have been uneven and lack strong enforcement mechanisms.[223]

Although Occupational Safety and Health Administration (OSHA) standards require employers to provide access to bathrooms in the workplace, OSHA also allows employers to create "reasonable restrictions" on bathroom usage – and

---

[223] M. Linder and I. Nygaard, *Void where prohibited: Rest breaks and the right to urinate on company time* (Ithaca: ILR Press, 1998).

reasonableness is to be evaluated on a case-by-case basis only if an employee makes a complaint to the Department of Labor.[224] With the exception of a few work categories where safety demands it – namely jobs like pilots and truck drivers – federal law does not require employers to provide rest breaks.[225] And, as of 2022, only eighteen states had statutes requiring employers to provide either meal or rest breaks of specified lengths and at specified intervals. Even those states with regulations on this topic sometimes include significant exceptions such as allowing employers to require employees to work through meal breaks or allowing them to avoid breaks all together if "a business necessity" requires it.[226] And, as Marc Linder and Ingrid Nygaard emphasize in their analysis of bathroom breaks, the need for an enforced legal right to use the bathroom at work is very unevenly distributed across job categories – office workers likely do not even think twice about bathroom breaks, while some factory workers are forced to use adult diapers to make it through the workday.[227]

Workplace regulations related to both physical bathroom access and the rest breaks needed to use a bathroom have particularly significant impacts on workers with marginalized identities. While access to public toilets is necessary for people to exist in the public sphere, access to adequate toilets in the workplace is necessary for access to employment opportunities. Workplace bathrooms intersect with issues like race, gender, and gender identity, as in the case of white workers striking to oppose integrated restroom facilities during World War II, discussed in Section 2.1. Workplaces and educational institutions have historically argued that a lack of women's restrooms meant it was not possible to admit or hire women.[228] And, in 2002, the Utah Transit Authority fired a trans bus driver on the basis that the UTA might face liability if the employee used a women's restroom while on her route. The UTA won a discrimination lawsuit in 2007, despite the fact that no one had even made a complaint about the employee's bathroom usage.[229]

---

[224] "U.S. Department of Labor – restrooms and sanitation requirements," 2023, accessed November 21, 2023, www.osha.gov/restrooms-sanitation. See in particular the letters of interpretation linked on this webpage.

[225] Linder and Nygaard, *Void where prohibited*, 9. See also Justia, "Meal and rest break laws in employment: 50-state survey," 2022, accessed November 21, 2023, www.justia.com/employ ment/employment-laws-50-state-surveys/meal-and-rest-break-laws-in-the-workplace-50-state-survey/.

[226] Justia, "Meal and rest break laws." Three additional states regulate meal or rest breaks but only for workers in specific industries, including retail (Maryland), factories (Nebraska), and agriculture (Pennsylvania).

[227] Linder and Nygaard, *Void where prohibited*, 2.   [228] Plaskow, "Embodiment," 53.

[229] *Etsitty v. Utah Transit Authority*, 502 F.3d 1215 (2007). P. Manson, "Appeals court upholds firing of transsexual," *Salt Lake Tribune (UT)*, September 22, 2007, https://infoweb.newsbank .com/apps/news/document-view?p=WORLDNEWS&docref=news/11BD3CBB1BC73C90, NewsBank.

Bathroom access also proves a significant challenge for employees who must rely on public facilities due to the variable location of their work. This includes individuals like cab drivers and street vendors as well as those working in the growing "gig" economy.[230] Women are particularly impacted by a lack of sufficient employer-provided restrooms, and may avoid these occupations all together or face sexual harassment as a result of inadequate facilities.[231] Some jurisdictions have begun to enact policies responding to the need for restroom access among mobile workers, although these are not yet comprehensive or widespread.[232]

6.2 Public Bathrooms and Homelessness

As discussed in more detail in Section 2.3, public investment in bathrooms waned in the 1920s.[233] In the modern period, concerns over terrorism, crime, and vandalism have led to even further decline in the availability of public toilets.[234] Instead, people out in public typically rely on private toilets located in businesses. The reliance on commercial, privately owned bathrooms to serve the public's needs is particularly problematic for unhoused individuals who do not have a home bathroom to fall back on and who may be refused by businesses because they are not customers or simply due to their appearance.[235]

Ron Hochbaum conducted a survey of city policies relating to bathrooms and homelessness in ten cities with the largest unhoused populations. He found that all ten cities criminalize public urination and defecation, with penalties ranging from fines to incarceration. At the same time, the provision of public bathrooms that are truly available to all populations is lacking. Ratios of public bathrooms to unhoused individuals ranged from 1:27 to 1:126, often falling below international requirements for refugee camps. And, of course, these bathrooms need to serve more than only the unhoused population and they are generally not open around

---

[230] L. Noren, "Only dogs are free to pee: New York cabbies' search for civility," in *Toilet: Public restrooms and the politics of sharing*, ed. H. Molotch and L. Noren (New York: New York University Press, 2010), 93–114.

[231] Noren, "Only dogs," 96; S. A. Moore, "Facility hostility? Sex discrimination and women's restrooms in the workplace," *Georgia Law Review* 36 (2002): 599–634. See also *DeClue v. Central Illinois Light Company* 223 F.3d 434 (2000), in which a federal court found in favor of the employer in a sexual harassment case involving inadequate provision of bathrooms for a female employee in a job without onsite bathrooms. See also on this topic Davis, *Bathroom battlegrounds*, 85–100.

[232] See, for example, "Drayage truck operators – Access to restroom facilities," Washington Laws of 2022, Chapter 204; "Agreements between third-party food delivery services and food service establishments and the provision of toilet facility access to food delivery workers," New York City Council, Law No. 2021/117 (2021).

[233] Baldwin, "Public privacy," 280.   [234] Banks, "Disappearing public toilet," 1063, 1073.

[235] Weinmeyer, "Lavatories," 418–424; E. Van Houweling and R. Botta, *Access to water and toilet facilities for the unhoused in Denver* (2023), 24, https://housekeysactionnetwork.com/wp-content/uploads/2023/09/WASH-Final-20230927.pdf.

the clock.[236] In a survey of people living unsheltered in Denver in 2023, Emily Van Houweling and Renée Botta found that over three-quarters reported serious challenges with locating a bathroom to use, and almost half regularly resorted to voiding without a toilet (either publicly or in a bag in their tent) as a result.[237]

The fact that criminalization of public urination/defecation is paired with a refusal to provide an alternative has both practical and psychological impacts on people experiencing homelessness. Hochbaum writes that in addition to serious public health consequences, "[t]he failure to provide public bathrooms is dehumanizing on its own and, when combined with prohibitions on bathroom functions, it signals to homeless individuals that society believes they should cease to exist."[238] The health and dignity issues associated with a lack of public bathrooms are exacerbated even further for unhoused people who menstruate and do not have adequate space and supplies to manage menstruation safely and hygienically.[239] Unsheltered women and disabled people of all genders face additional barriers due to more frequent needs to access bathroom facilities, inaccessible facilities that are not ADA-compliant, and serious safety concerns around the use of public facilities.[240]

6.3 Toilets and Sanitation in Global Context

Toilets as a political issue and signifier of social citizenship is not unique to the United States. Dating back to the early twentieth century, city leaders on multiple continents struggled with the growing presence of women in the public sphere and what that might mean for public bathroom provision and design.[241] And, in the present day, countries around the world are grappling with many of the same policy issues that we see being debated in state legislatures.

For example, advocacy around universal changing stations began first in the UK and Australia with the Changing Places organizations.[242] In 2020, Scotland

---

[236] R. S. Hochbaum, "Bathrooms as a homeless rights issue," *North Carolina Law Review* 98, no. 2 (2020): 205–272. Some public bathrooms, such as those in parks, may also be closed for several months during the winter.

[237] Van Houweling and Botta, *Access*, 13, 18.

[238] Hochbaum, "Bathrooms as a homeless rights issue," 208.

[239] H. Teizazu, M. Sommer, C. Gruer, et al., "'Do we not bleed?' Sanitation, menstrual management, and homelessness in the time of covid," *Columbia Journal of Gender and Law* 41 (2021): 238–244; A. Sebert Kuhlmann, E. Peters Bergquist, D. Danjoint, and L. L. Wall, "Unmet menstrual hygiene needs among low-income women," *Obstetrics & Gynecology* 133, no. 2 (2019), https://journals.lww.com/greenjournal/fulltext/2019/02000/unmet_menstrual_hygiene_needs_among_low_income.2.aspx; Van Houweling and Botta, *Access*, 23.

[240] Van Houweling and Botta, *Access*, 22–23.

[241] Flanagan, "Private needs."; Cooper, Law, Malthus, and Wood, "Rooms of their own."

[242] "Changing Places toilets," 2023, accessed November 21, 2023, www.changing-places.org/; BBC, "Changing Places toilets for disabled people to be compulsory," July 18, 2020, www.bbc.com/news/uk-england-53448846; "Changing Places transforming lives," 2023, accessed November 21, 2023,

became the first country to pass legislation requiring the government to provide free menstrual products to anyone who needs them, and other countries are considering similar measures or already ensure access in specific locations like schools.[243] Support for the use of bathrooms consistent with gender identity varies widely across the globe. In a twenty-three-country survey in 2016, researchers at UCLA's Williams Institute found that respondents in Spain, Argentina, and India were the most supportive of trans people using restrooms according to gender identity, while those in Russia were the most opposed by far (only 26 percent strongly or somewhat supported bathroom access for trans people, compared to around 40 percent for the next-least-supportive country, China).[244]

Of course, some countries more deeply impacted by poverty face much more basic and serious challenges with regard to toilet access as compared to the United States. In the developing world, issues of toilet access are very different, in that many people lack access to sanitary toilet facilities not just in public spaces but altogether. The United Nations includes access to clean water and sanitation in its Sustainable Development Goals, and estimates that as of 2022, about 43 percent of the world's population lacked access to safely managed sanitation.[245]

The movement for safe and sanitary toilets in the Global South has been particularly active in India, where the Supreme Court of India is unique in being the only nation to explicitly find a right to sanitation to be protected by its national constitution.[246] Two city courts within India have even ruled that there is a constitutional requirement for the government to provide clean, publicly available bathrooms.[247] And, issues of class and identity remain intertwined. The Indian city cases in particular focused on the needs of female residents for sanitary bathroom facilities, both from a dignity perspective and a safety

https://changingplaces.org.au/; Australian Department of Social Services, "Disability and carers: Changing Spaces," 2023, accessed November 21, 2023, www.dss.gov.au/disability-and-carers-programs-services/changing-places.

[243] R. Tumin, "Scotland makes period products free," *The New York Times*, August 15, 2022, www.nytimes.com/2022/08/15/world/europe/scotland-free-period-products.html.

[244] A. R. Flores, T. N. T. Brown, and A. S. Park, *Public support for transgender rights: A twenty-three country survey*, UCLA School of Law Williams Institute (2016), https://williamsinstitute.law.ucla.edu/publications/trans-rights-23-country-survey/. See also L. M. Lombrana, "Spain's win for transgender rights almost tore the country apart," *Bloomberg*, December 22, 2022, https://search-ebscohost-com.du.idm.oclc.org/login.aspx?direct=true&db=bth&AN=160933136&site=ehost-live&scope=site.

[245] *The Sustainable Development Goals report*, United Nations (2023), https://unstats.un.org/sdgs/report/2023/The-Sustainable-Development-Goals-Report-2023.pdf. See also C. McFarlane, *Waste and the city: The crisis of sanitation and the right to citylife* (Verso, 2023), 221.

[246] Weinmeyer, "Lavatories," 447.   [247] Weinmeyer, "Lavatories," 449–450.

perspective – open defecation exposes women and girls to a high risk of assault, especially for those among lower castes.[248] The women-led Right to Pee movement in India emphasizes themes connected to social citizenship explicitly. In interviews with Colin McFarlane, activists with Right to Pee argued that campaigns around safe and equal toilets are "about the 'freedom' to participate in the city, to move around and not be stuck indoors, and repeatedly asserted that the struggle was about 'citizenship': 'It's not about facilities, it's a political statement.'"[249]

6.4 Bathrooms and Democracy

Indeed, access to toilets is a political issue, and one that is deeply intertwined with democracy. The central question of this Element is what connects seemingly disparate policies that impact different identities and aspects of restroom access. I argue that social citizenship helps explain why bathrooms are so important to accessing public spaces, as well as why they have been such frequent targets for exclusion and symbols of inclusion in the US history and contemporary politics.

In some situations, the right of targeted groups to exist in society fully as themselves has become a hotly contested political and partisan issue. In these cases, both the physical denial of access to bathrooms and severe harms to dignity can result when those in power are able to use bathroom-related policies as a way to define the boundaries of full citizenship. In other cases, the battle is one of being seen and recognized as politically relevant in the first place. For example, when considering a policy like universal changing stations, many in power may not have ever thought about the group that requires an adult changing table for access, much less considered them a constituency worth investing political capital in. Here, belongingness is allocated only when individuals and groups are able to be seen and recognized.

These forces all become magnified in our federal system, where not just policies but democratization itself is uneven across the states. Phil Rocco writes that "the foundations of democratic rule – free and fair elections, competitive

---

[248] Weinmeyer, "Lavatories," 449–450; R. Pacheco-Vega, "Towards a holistic understanding of sanitation: The links between menstrual hygiene management, open defecation and violence against women," May 31, 2014, www.raulpacheco.org/2014/05/towards-a-holistic-understanding-of-sanitation-the-links-between-menstrual-hygiene-management-open-defecation-and-violence-against-women/; L. Bliss, "The lack of equal bathroom access for women is a global design flaw," *Reuters/Bloomberg*, November 7, 2014, www.bloomberg.com/news/articles/2014-11-07/the-lack-of-equal-bathroom-access-for-women-is-a-global-design-flaw. See also McFarlane, *Waste and the city*, 36–41 on gender and sanitation globally.

[249] McFarlane, *Waste and the city*, 25.

parties, and institutional support for civil and social rights – are not even across the fifty states."[250] This is particularly true when it comes to policies focused on gender identity. States that have enacted trans-exclusionary bathroom bills rank significantly lower, on average, on a measure of state-level democracy developed by Jake Grumbach.[251]

In extreme cases, trans-exclusionary bathroom bills, especially in conjunction with other legislation targeting trans people, can drive people out of their home state all together. For example, Devin Myers, a trans college student, moved away from Florida after the state passed a bathroom bill making using the "wrong" bathroom a misdemeanor – specifically, she feared that using the restroom while protesting at the state capital could lead to her arrest.[252] On an individual level, these decisions to relocate may be rational and even necessary. But, in the aggregate, trans adults and the families of trans kids moving out of states with anti-trans legislation then changes the organizing and political landscape in the future. There are fewer state citizens willing to testify at state legislative hearings and fewer voters who might cast their ballot with these issues at front of mind, creating a negative feedback loop.

Denying toilet access means that individuals can only exist in public for as long as they can "hold it." Bathroom policies can set both a biological limit and a psychological one on access to education, employment, social, and political participation. Thus, ensuring equal access to bathrooms – or denying it to disfavored groups – becomes a powerful way for society to define who is a full citizen and to indicate who belongs and who doesn't in public spaces, with important implications for democracy.

---

[250] P. Rocco, "Laboratories of what? American federalism and the politics of democratic subversion," in *Democratic resilience: Can the US withstand rising polarization?* ed. R. Lieberman, S. Mettler, and K. Roberts (New York: Cambridge University Press, 2021), 310.

[251] More details on the State Democracy Index can be found in J. M. Grumbach, "Laboratories of democratic backsliding," *American Political Science Review* 117, no. 3 (2023): 967–984. I use the main State Democracy Index measure for 2018 (the latest date available) in this calculation. I conducted a t-test of the average state-level democracy index score for states that have enacted a trans-exclusionary bathroom bill versus those that have not (t-test for difference; diff $= -.81$, $t = 2.22$, $p = 0.03$).

[252] F. Latifi, "Trans youth are moving from states with anti-trans laws in search of safety, health care," *Teen Vogue*, August 3, 2023, www.teenvogue.com/story/trans-youth-moving-states-anti-trans-laws. See also B. Kennerley, "Brevard families leaving Florida: Why they say Sunshine State no longer feels like home," *Florida Today*, May 31, 2023, www.floridatoday.com/story/news/2023/05/31/families-leave-florida-desantis-laws-lgbtq-transgender-rights-immigration/70215225007/.

Data Appendix

Identifying relevant statutes involved searching news sources, state legislative websites, and LegiScan (https://legiscan.com/). In some policy areas where interest groups or businesses track policy enactment, I was able to start with a list or map of statutes, which I then confirmed and often expanded using government sources (i.e. state legislative websites, and statute books). These interest group lists included:

Policy	Interest group or business group	Link (most recent update dates vary)
Ally's Law	Crohn's & Colitis Foundation	www.crohnscolitisfoundation .org/get-involved/be-an-advocate/restroom-access
Trans-Exclusionary Bathroom Bills	Movement Advancement Project	www.lgbtmap.org/equality-maps/nondiscrimination/ bathroom_bans
Universal Changing Stations	CAN-DAN (adult changing table manufacturer)	www.can-dan.com/ legislation/
Baby Changing Tables in Men's Rooms	Koala Care (baby changing table manufacturer)	www.koalabear.com/product-resources/changing-station-resources-landing-page/com pliance-homepage/legisla tion-map/
Menstrual Products in Schools	Women's Voices for the Earth	https://womensvoices.org/ 2022/05/02/sixty-two-men strual-equity-laws-passed-in-the-united-states/
Menstrual Products in Prisons	Prison Flow Project	https://theprisonflowproject .com/state-laws-around-access

Data on votes and legislator partisanship was collected primarily from LegiScan (https://legiscan.com/). In some cases, this data was supplemented with information from state legislature websites and online legislative journals, as well as partisanship data from Boris Shor and Nolan McCarthy.[1]

---

[1] B. Shor and N. McCarty, "The ideological mapping of American legislatures," *American Political Science Review* 105, no. 3 (2011): 530–551; B. Shor, "Individual state legislator Shor-McCarty ideology data, July 2020 update" (V1: Harvard Dataverse, 2020), https://doi.org/10.7910/DVN/ GZJOT3.

Bibliography

"2018 – Statewide – Question 3." Secretary of the Commonwealth of Massa chusetts, 2018, accessed March 2, 2023, https://electionstats.state.ma.us/bal lot_questions/view/7305/.

"About Freedom for All Massachusetts." 2018, accessed March 2, 2023, https:// web.archive.org/web/20180528214716/https://www.freedommassachusetts .org/about/.

ACLU National Prison Project. *Menstrual equity: A legislative toolkit*. American Civil Liberties Union, 2019.

Ali, D. "The rise and fall of the bathroom bill: State legislation affecting trans & gender non-binary people," *NASPA, Student Affairs Administrators in Higher Education*, April 2, 2019, www.naspa.org/blog/the-rise-and-fall-of-the-bath room-bill-state-legislation-affecting-trans-and-gender-non-binary-people.

American Legislative Exchange Council. "Dignity for incarcerated women." 2018, accessed November 27, 2023, https://alec.org/model-policy/dignity-for-incarcerated-women/.

Anthony, K. H., and M. Dufresne. "Potty privileging in perspective: Gender and family issues." In *Ladies and gents: Public toilets and gender*, edited by O. Gershenson and B. Penner. Philadelphia: Temple University Press, 2009, 48–61.

Aukett, L. "One voice makes a difference." *Ostomy Quarterly* 43, no. 1 (2005): 67.

Australian Department of Social Services. "Disability and carers: Changing Spaces." 2023, accessed November 21, 2023, www.dss.gov.au/disability-and-carers-programs-services/changing-places.

Bagagli, B. P., T. V. Chaves, and M. G. Zoppi Fontana. "Trans women and public restrooms: The legal discourse and its violence." *Frontiers in Sociology* 6 (2021): 1–14.

Baldwin, P. C. "Public privacy: Restrooms in American cities, 1869–1932." *Journal of Social History* 48, no. 2 (2014): 264–288.

Banks, T. L. "The disappearing public toilet." *Seton Hall Law Review* 50, no. 4 (2019): 1061–1094.

Barnett, B. S., A. E. Nesbit, and R. M. Sorrentino. "The transgender bathroom debate at the intersection of politics, law, ethics, and science." *The Journal of the American Academy of Psychiatry and the Law* 46, no. 2 (2018): 232–241.

A bathroom's standard changing table doesn't fit families with special needs, Aired May 28, 2021, on 9News. www.9news.com/video/news/local/next/

bathrooms-changing-table-families-special-needs/73-9d380ca3-cc1d-40af-8d3c-09ea893f748e.

BBC. "Changing places toilets for disabled people to be compulsory." July 18, 2020. www.bbc.com/news/uk-england-53448846.

Bedigan, M. "Ten-year-old boy gets harsh sentence for public urination." *The Independent*, December 14, 2023. www.the-independent.com/news/world/americas/crime/boy-sentence-public-urination-b2464417.html.

Béland, D. "The social exclusion discourse: Ideas and policy change." *Policy & Politics* 35, no. 1 (2007): 123–139.

Bever, L. "'As if we don't exist': Frustrated father pleads for more changing tables in men's restrooms." *Washington Post*, October 3, 2018. www.washingtonpost.com/news/parenting/wp/2018/10/03/as-if-we-dont-exist-frustrated-father-pleads-for-more-changing-tables-in-mens-restrooms/.

Bliss, L. "The lack of equal bathroom access for women is a global design flaw." *Reuters/Bloomberg*, November 7, 2014. www.bloomberg.com/news/articles/2014-11-07/the-lack-of-equal-bathroom-access-for-women-is-a-global-design-flaw.

Bloemraad, I., W. Kymlicka, M. Lamont, and L. S. S. Hing. "Membership without social citizenship? Deservingness & redistribution as grounds for equality." *Daedalus* 148, no. 3 (2019): 73–104.

Blossom, V. T. *It has happened here*. New York: Harper, 1959.

Bohnel, S. "Advocates speak in favor of bill establishing gender-inclusive restrooms in county buildings, certain businesses." *Bethesda Magazine*, March 9, 2022. https://bethesdamagazine.com/bethesda-beat/government/advocates-speak-in-favor-of-bill-establishing-gender-inclusive-restrooms-in-county-buildings-certain-businesses/.

Boris, E. "'You wouldn't want one of 'em dancing with your wife': Racialized bodies on the job in World War II." *American Quarterly* 50, no. 1 (1998): 77–108.

Branigin, A., and N. Kirkpatrick. "Anti-trans laws are on the rise. Here's a look at where – and what kind." *Washington Post*, October 14, 2022. www.washingtonpost.com/lifestyle/2022/10/14/anti-trans-bills/.

Brodie, L. F. *Breaking out: VMI and the coming of women*. New York: Pantheon Books, 2000.

Burgdorf Jr., R. L., "Equal members of the community: The public accommodations provisions of the Americans with Disabilities Act." *Temple Law Review* 64, no. 2 (1991): 551–582.

Burns, K. "The bathroom bill era is over." *Medium*, June 30, 2021. https://katelynburns.medium.com/the-bathroom-bill-era-is-over-ed0018b44441.

California Legislative Information. "AB-1266 pupil rights: Sex-segregated school programs and activities." 2013, accessed March 1, 2023, https://leginfo.legis lature.ca.gov/faces/billTextClient.xhtml?bill_id=201320140AB1266.

Call, J. "A mom's mission: Bill seeks to require adult changing tables in Florida public restrooms." *Tallahasee Democrat*, December 25, 2019. www.talla hassee.com/story/news/politics/2019/12/09/bill-seeks-require-adult-chan ging-tables-florida-public-restrooms/4354123002/.

"Changing Places toilets." 2023, accessed November 21, 2023, www.changing-places.org/.

"Changing Places transforming lives." 2023, accessed November 21, 2023, https://changingplaces.org.au/.

"Changing Spaces campaign." 2023, accessed November 15, 2023, www.chan gingspacescampaign.com/.

"Changing Spaces campaign – Ohio chapter." 2023, accessed November 15, 2023, www.changingspacescampaign.com/ohio.

Cimo, A. *AB 283 Alex Cimo testimony.* Nevada: Nevada State Assembly, Committee of Health and Human Services, 2021.

Cline, N. "Virginia rules commission objects to proposed transgender policies." *Virginia Mercury*, December 19, 2022. www.virginiamercury.com/2022/ 12/19/virginia-rules-commission-objects-to-proposed-transgender-pol icies/.

Colker, R. "Public restrooms: Flipping the default rules." *Ohio State Law Journal* 78, no. 1 (2017): 145–180.

"Concord mom receives advocacy award, state assembly recognition for work on successful adult changing table bill." *Family Voices of California*, June 28, 2016, www.familyvoicesofca.org/adult-changing-tables-federal-autism-panel-bleeding-disorders/.

Congress.gov. "Actions overview: H.R.5147 – 114th Congress (2015–2016)." 2016, accessed November 8, 2023, www.congress.gov/bill/114th-con gress/house-bill/5147/actions.

"Actions overview: S.756 – 115th Congress (2017–2018)." 2018, accessed November 10, 2023, www.congress.gov/bill/115th-congress/senate-bill/ 756/actions.

"H.R.3646 – Menstrual Equity for All Act of 2023." 2023, accessed November 7, 2023, www.congress.gov/bill/118th-congress/house-bill/3646.

Conlon, R. "Will strict new anti-trans laws in Kansas keep people and compan ies away?" *KMUW Wichita*, May 3, 2023. www.kmuw.org/news/2023-05-03/kansas-anti-transgender-law-bathroom-bill-athletes-gender.

Cook, T. M. "The Americans with Disabilities Act: The move to integration." *Temple Law Review* 64, no. 2 (1991): 393–470.

Cooper, A., R. Law, J. Malthus, and P. Wood. "Rooms of their own: Public toilets and gendered citizens in a New Zealand city, 1860–1940." *Gender, Place and Culture: A Journal of Feminist Geography* 7, no. 4 (2000): 417–433.

Cooper, E. B. "What's law got to do with it? Dignity and menstruation." *Columbia Journal of Gender and Law* 41 (2021): 39–52.

Cooper, R., C. Heldman, A. R. Ackerman, and V. A. Farrar-Meyers. "Hidden corporate profits in the US prison system: The unorthodox policy-making of the American Legislative Exchange Council." *Contemporary Justice Review* 19, no. 3 (2016): 380–400.

Crawford, B. J., M. E. Johnson, M. L. Karin, L. Strausfeld, and E. G. Waldman. "The ground on which we all stand: A conversation about menstrual equity law and activism." *Michigan Journal of Gender & Law* 26, no. 2 (2019): 341–388.

Crays, A. "Menstrual equity and justice in the United States." *Sexuality, Gender, and Policy* 3 (2020): 134–147.

Darivemula, S., A. Knittel, L. Flowers, et al. "Menstrual equity in the criminal legal system." *Journal of Women's Health* 32, no. 9 (2023): 927–931.

Davis, A. K. *Bathroom battlegrounds: How public restrooms shape the gender order.* Oakland: University of California Press, 2020.

Davis, H. F. "Why the 'transgender' bathroom controversy should make us rethink sex-segregated public bathrooms." *Politics, Groups, and Identities* 6, no. 2 (2018): 199–216.

Davis, L. J. *Enabling acts: The hidden story of how the Americans with Disabilities Act gave the largest US minority its rights.* Boston: Beacon Press, 2015.

"Design Approaches presents the pros and cons of the three most common solutions to all-gender restrooms: The single, multi-unit, and low-budget retrofit solution." 2023, accessed July 7, 2023, www.stalled.online/ approaches.

Dura, J., J. Hanna, and S. Murphy. "In some states with laws on transgender bathrooms, officials may not know how they will be enforced." *Associated Press*, June 25, 2023. https://apnews.com/article/transgender-bathroom-laws-enforcement-e96e94b8935eb6bd23a42562cdeeec6c.

Dwyer, P. *Understanding social citizenship: Themes and perspectives for policy and practice.* Bristol: The Policy Press, 2004.

Elwood, K. "Va. killed bills aimed at trans youths. Here's where the debate moves next." *Washington Post*, March 1, 2023. www.washingtonpost .com/education/2023/03/01/virginia-education-transgender-youth/.

"What to know about Virginia's transgender student model policies." *Washington Post*, August 18, 2023. www.washingtonpost.com/educa tion/2023/07/23/virginia-transgender-model-policies-faq/.

Fettig, A. "Menstrual equity, organizing and the struggle for human dignity and gender equality in prison." *Columbia Journal of Gender and Law* 41 (2021): 76–99.

Flanagan, M. "Private needs, public space: Public toilets provision in the Anglo-Atlantic patriarchal city: London, Dublin, Toronto and Chicago." *Urban History* 41, no. 2 (2014): 265–290.

Flores, A. R., T. N. T. Brown, and A. S. Park. *Public support for transgender rights: A twenty-three country survey.* Los Angeles: UCLA School of Law Williams Institute, 2016. https://williamsinstitute.law.ucla.edu/publications/trans-rights-23-country-survey/.

Crohn's and Colitis Foundation, "Restroom Access Act (model legislation)." 2019, accessed June 28, 2022, www.crohnscolitisfoundation.org/sites/default/files/2019-10/Restroom%20Access%20model%20legislation.docx.pdf.

Francis, L., S. Meraj, D. Konduru, and E. M. Perrin. "An update on state legislation supporting menstrual hygiene products in US schools: A legislative review, policy report, and recommendations for school nurse leadership." *The Journal of School Nursing* 39, no. 6 (2023): 536–541.

Fraser, N., and L. Gordon. "Contract versus charity: Why is there no social citizenship in the United States?" *Socialist Review* 22, no. 3 (1993): 45–67.

Gabriel, T. "Two families got fed up with their states' politics: So they moved out." *New York Times*, October 7, 2023. www.nytimes.com/2023/10/07/us/politics/politics-states-moving.html.

Gash, A., D. Tichenor, A. Chavez, and M. Musselman. "Framing kids: Children, immigration reform, and same-sex marriage." *Politics, Groups, and Identities* 8, no. 1 (2020): 44–70.

Gill-Peterson, J. *Histories of the transgender child.* Minneapolis: University of Minnesota Press, 2018.

Godfrey, P. "Bayonets, brainwashing, and bathrooms: The discourse of race, gender, and sexuality in the desegregation of Little Rock's Central High." *The Arkansas Historical Quarterly* 62, no. 1 (2003): 42–67.

Gordon, J. "A 10-year-old in Mississippi who was arrested for urinating in public gets probation and a book report assignment." *CNN*, December 13, 2023. www.cnn.com/2023/12/13/us/mississippi-boy-arrested-urinating-book-report/index.html.

Greed, C. "Creating a nonsexist restroom." In *Toilet: Public restrooms and the politics of sharing*, edited by H. Molotch and L. Noren, 117–141. New York: New York University Press, 2010.

Green, E. L. "New Biden rules would bar discrimination against transgender students." *The New York Times*, June 23, 2022. www.nytimes.com/2022/06/23/us/politics/biden-transgender-students-discrimination.html.

Grumbach, J. M. *Laboratories against democracy: How national parties transformed state politics*. Princeton: Princeton University Press, 2022.

"Laboratories of democratic backsliding." *American Political Science Review* 117, no. 3 (2023): 967–984.

Hasenbush, A., A. R. Flores, and J. L. Herman. "Gender identity nondiscrimination laws in public accommodations: A review of evidence regarding safety and privacy in public restrooms, locker rooms, and changing rooms." *Sexuality Research and Social Policy* 16, no. 1 (2019): 70–83.

Haven, K. "Why I'm fighting for menstrual equity in prison." *ACLU News & Commentary*, November 8, 2019. www.aclu.org/news/prisoners-rights/why-im-fighting-for-menstrual-equity-in-prison.

Hertel-Fernandez, A. "Who passes business's 'model bills'? Policy capacity and corporate influence in US state politics." *Perspectives on Politics* 12, no. 3 (2014): 582–602.

Hochbaum, R. S. "Bathrooms as a homeless rights issue." *North Carolina Law Review* 98, no. 2 (2020): 205–272.

Hoy, S. *Chasing dirt: The American pursuit of cleanliness*. New York: Oxford University Press, 1997.

Huh, W. T., J. Lee, H. Park, and K. S. Park. "The potty parity problem: Towards gender equality at restrooms in business facilities." *Socio-Economic Planning Sciences* 68 (2019): 1–10.

Iafolla, R., and J. E. Moreno. "Federal judge topples EEOC's LGBT bathroom, pronoun guidance." *Bloomberg Law*, October 3, 2022. https://news.bloomberglaw.com/daily-labor-report/federal-judge-topples-eeocs-lgbt-bathroom-and-pronoun-guidance.

International Code Council. "International Plumbing Code (IPC)." International Code Council, 2023, accessed February 13, 2023, www.iccsafe.org/content/international-plumbing-code-ipc-home-page/.

"International Code Council: Code adoptions." 2023, accessed November 28, 2023, www.iccsafe.org/advocacy/#code-adoption-database.

"International Plumbing Code changes facilitate all-gender restrooms." *The Architect's Newspaper*, March 27, 2019. www.archpaper.com/2019/03/international-plumbing-code-changes-facilitate-all-gender-restrooms/.

Johnson, M. "Before its time: Public perception of disability rights, the Americans with Disabilities Act, and the future of access and accommodation disabilities." *Washington University Journal of Law & Policy* 23 (2007): 121–150.

Vermont. *Journal of the House*. 2017. https://legislature.vermont.gov/ Documents/2018/Docs/JOURNAL/hj170421.pdf.

Justia. "Meal and rest break laws in employment: 50-state survey." 2022, accessed November 21, 2023, www.justia.com/employment/employ ment-laws-50-state-surveys/meal-and-rest-break-laws-in-the-workplace-50-state-survey/.

Kanter, A. S. "The Americans with Disabilities Act at 25 years: Lessons to learn from the convention on the rights of people with disabilities." *Drake Law Review* 63, no. 3 (2015): 819–884.

Kennerley, B. "Brevard families leaving Florida: Why they say Sunshine State no longer feels like home." *Florida Today*, May 31, 2023. www.floridato day.com/story/news/2023/05/31/families-leave-florida-desantis-laws-lgbtq-transgender-rights-immigration/70215225007/.

King, D. "ODOT adding adult-sized changing tables in 28 highway rest areas by 2026." *Columbus Dispatch*, May 13, 2023. www.dispatch.com/story/ news/healthcare/2023/05/18/odot-adding-adult-sized-changing-tables-in-28-highway-rest-areas-universal-disability/70205223007/.

"Koala Kare: Dads for change." 2022, www.koalabear.com/parent-resources/ dads-for-change/.

Kogan, T. S. "Public restrooms and the distorting of transgender identity." *North Carolina Law Review* 95, no. 4 (2016): 1205–1239.

"Sex-separation in public restrooms: Law, architecture, and gender." *Michigan Journal of Gender & Law* 14, no. 1 (2007): 1–57.

"Sex separation: The cure-all for Victorian social anxiety." In *Toilet: Public restrooms and the politics of sharing*, edited by H. Molotch and L. Noren, 145–164. New York: New York University Press, 2010.

Kurtz, J. "Congressional Dads Caucus calls for more baby changing stations in Capitol complex." *The Hill*, April 28, 2023. https://thehill.com/blogs/in-the-know/3978018-congressional-dads-caucus-calls-for-more-baby-chan ging-stations-in-capitol-complex/.

Kutcher, A. "Change.Org: Stop gender stereotyping: Provide universally accessible changing tables in all your stores." 2015, accessed December 19, 2022, www .change.org/p/bethechange-provide-universally-accessible-changing-tables-in-all-your-stores?utm_source=Aplus&utm_medium=website&utm_ campaign=bethechange.

Laird, J. F. "Argentine, Kansas: The evolution of a Mexican American commu-nity, 1905–1940." PhD Thesis, University of Kansas, 1975.

Lane, B., A. Perez-Brumer, R. Parker, A. Sprong, and M. Sommer. "Improving menstrual equity in the USA: Perspectives from trans and non-binary people assigned female at birth and health care providers." *Culture, Health & Sexuality* 24, no. 10 (2022): 1408–1422.

Larimer, S. "Ashton Kutcher just wants to change his kid's diaper, man." *Washington Post*, March 25, 2015. www.washingtonpost.com/news/par enting/wp/2015/03/25/ashton-kutcher-just-wants-to-change-his-kids-dia per-man/.

Latifi, F. "Trans youth are moving from states with anti-trans laws in search of safety, health care." *Teen Vogue*, August 3, 2023. www.teenvogue.com/ story/trans-youth-moving-states-anti-trans-laws.

Lerner, R. H. "Recognizing menstrual equity as a dimension of equal educational opportunity." *Journal of Law & Education* 52, no. 1 (2023): 226–263.

Lewis, M. M., and S. E. Eckes. "Storytelling, leadership, and the law: Using amicus briefs to understand the impact of school district policies and practices related to transgender student inclusion." *Educational Administration Quarterly* 56, no. 1 (2020): 46–88.

Linder, M., and I. Nygaard. *Void where prohibited: Rest breaks and the right to urinate on company time*. Ithaca: ILR Press, 1998.

Lister, R. "Inclusive citizenship: Realizing the potential." *Citizenship Studies* 11, no. 1 (2007): 49–61.

Littlefield, S. "Adult changing tables are now Minnesota law in all new public restrooms." *WCCO News*, May 30, 2023. www.cbsnews.com/minnesota/ news/adult-changing-tables-are-now-minnesota-law-in-all-new-public- restrooms/.

Liversedge, J. "Rest areas: Intersections of the American experience." MA Thesis, University of Michigan-Flint, 2022.

Loller, T. "Transgender child sues over Tennessee school bathroom law." *Associated Press*, August 4, 2022. https://apnews.com/article/sports-educa tion-lawsuits-tennessee-nashville-e2ec93649389e5b74e191066bd3cd956.

Lombrana, L. M. "Spain's win for transgender rights almost tore the country apart." *Bloomberg*, December 22, 2022. https://search-ebscohost-com.du.idm.oclc .org/login.aspx?direct=true&db=bth&AN=160933136&site=ehost- live&scope=site.

"Love the change: Pampers, Koala Kare to install 5,000 changing tables in men's restrooms across U.S. and Canada." *ABC7*, June 12, 2019. https://abc7chi cago.com/pampers-love-for-change-john-legend-donte-palmer/5343179/.

Lowery, M. M. *Lumbee Indians in the Jim Crow south: Race, identity, and the making of a nation*. Chapel Hill: The University of North Carolina Press, 2010.

Manson, P. "Appeals court upholds firing of transsexual." *Salt Lake Tribune (UT)*, September 22, 2007. https://infoweb.newsbank.com/apps/news/

document-view?p=WORLDNEWS&docref=news/11BD3CBB1BC73C90. NewsBank.

Marshall, T. H., and T. Bottomore. *Citizenship and social class*. London: Pluto Press, 1992.

Martin, K., and E. Rahilly. "Value frames in discourse supporting transgender athlete bans." *Discourse & Society* 34, no. 6 (2023): 732–751.

Maryland General Assembly. "Health and Government Operations – witness list." 2021, accessed November 29, 2023, https://mgaleg.maryland.gov/ mgawebsite/Legislation/WitnessSignup/HB0321?ys=2021RS.

McFarlane, C. *Waste and the city: The crisis of sanitation and the right to citylife*. London: Verso, 2023.

Michaels, S. "We tracked down the lawyers behind the recent wave of anti-trans bathroom bills." *Mother Jones*, April 25, 2016. www.motherjones.com/ politics/2016/04/alliance-defending-freedom-lobbies-anti-lgbt-bathroom- bills/.

Millar, J. "Social exclusion and social policy research: Defining exclusion." In *Multidisciplinary handbook of social exclusion research*, edited by D. Abrams, J. Christian, and D. Gordon, 1–15. New York: John Wiley & Sons, 2008.

Missouri Appleseed. *Research summary: Access to menstrual hygiene products in Missouri prisons*, 2023, https://missouriappleseed.org/wp-content/ uploads/2023/06/23_MoApp_Menstrual-Hyg-Research.pdf.

Montano, E. "The bring your own tampon policy: Why menstrual hygiene products should be provided for free in restrooms." *University of Miami Law Review* 73, no. 1 (2018): 370–411.

Moore, S. A. "Facility hostility? Sex discrimination and women's restrooms in the workplace." *Georgia Law Review* 36 (2002): 599–634.

Movement Advancement Project. "Bans on transgender youth participation in sports." 2023, accessed July 7, 2023, www.lgbtmap.org/equality-maps/ sports_participation_bans.

"Health care laws and policies." 2023, accessed August 17, 2023, www .lgbtmap.org/equality-maps/healthcare_laws_and_policies/youth_medical_ care_bans.

"Nondiscrimination laws." 2023, accessed July 7, 2023, www.lgbtmap.org/ equality-maps/non_discrimination_laws/public-accommodations.

"Safe schools laws." 2023, accessed July 7, 2023, www.lgbtmap.org/equal ity-maps/safe_school_laws/discrimination.

Natanson, H. "Should there be diaper-changing stations in men's bathrooms? With proposed new law, D.C. wades into national debate." *Washington Post*, July 14, 2019. www.washingtonpost.com/local/social-issues/should-there-be-diaper-changing-stations-in-mens-bathrooms-with-proposed-law-dc-wades-into-national-debate/2019/07/14/72c800f6-9cc8-11e9-85d6-5211733f92c7_story.html.

"Virginia policy latest attempt to restrict rights of transgender students." *Washington Post*, September 17, 2022. www.washingtonpost.com/educa tion/2022/09/16/trans-students-virginia-bathroom-sports/.

"Virginia school board will pay $1.3 million in settlement to transgender student Gavin Grimm, who sued over bathroom policy." *Washington Post*, August 26, 2021. www.washingtonpost.com/local/education/transgender-bathroom-settlement-gavin-grimm/2021/08/26/0f186784-0699-11ec-a266-7c7fe02fa374_story.html.

Noren, L. "Only dogs are free to pee: New York cabbies' search for civility." In *Toilet: Public restrooms and the politics of sharing*, edited by H. Molotch and L. Noren, 93–114. New York: New York University Press, 2010.

Norton, M. J. "Testimony of Michael J. Norton; senior counsel, Alliance Defending Freedom." Alliance Defending Freedom, Updated February 14, 2015, accessed June 29, 2022, www.leg.state.co.us/CLICS/CLICS2015A/comm summ.nsf/b4a3962433b52fa787256e5f00670a71/4f3a48ec0a54330687257 de2005e3f8c/%24FILE/15HouseState0204AttachC.pdf#page=5.

Owens, S. "The grassroots movement to change the nation's public restroom laws." *US News & World Report*, December 20, 2012. www.usnews.com/ news/articles/2012/12/20/the-grassroots-movement-to-change-the-nations-public-restroom-laws.

Pacheco-Vega, R., "Towards a holistic understanding of sanitation: The links between menstrual hygiene management, open defecation and violence against women." May 31, 2014, www.raulpacheco.org/2014/05/towards-a-holistic-understanding-of-sanitation-the-links-between-menstrual-hygiene-management-open-defecation-and-violence-against-women/.

Palmer, Donte. "Squat for change." 2022, https://squatforchange.com/.

Pandya, Nishant, Rachel Granberg, and McIntire Russel K. "A method for investigating access to diaper changing stations in restaurants." *Cureus* 13, no. 10 (2021): 1–6.

Peters, J. W., J. Becker, and J. H. Davis. "Trump rescinds rules on bathrooms for transgender students." *The New York Times*, February 22, 2017. www .nytimes.com/2017/02/22/us/politics/devos-sessions-transgender-students-rights.html.

Pickerill, J. M., and C. J. Bowling. "Polarized parties, politics, and policies: Fragmented federalism in 2013–2014." *Publius: The Journal of Federalism* 44, no. 3 (2014): 369–398.

Planas, A. "Race played role in sentencing of black child, 10, for urinating in public, lawyer says." *NBC News*, December 13, 2023. www.nbcnews.com/news/nbcblk/race-played-role-sentencing-black-child-10-urinating-public-lawyer-say-rcna129631.

Plaskow, J. "Embodiment, elimination, and the role of toilets in struggles for social justice." *CrossCurrents* 58, no. 1 (2008): 51–64.

Progressive Urban Management Associates. *City of Denver public restrooms pilot project*. Denver, 2018.

Raffa, M. F. "Removing architectural barriers: The Architectural Barriers Act of 1968." *Mental and Physical Disability Law Reporter* 9, no. 4 (1985): 304–308.

"Restroom access." Crohn's and Colitis Foundation, 2022, accessed June 28, 2022, www.crohnscolitisfoundation.org/get-involved/be-an-advocate/restroom-access.

Ring, T. "California adopts groundbreaking all-gender restroom access law." *The Advocate*, September 29, 2016. www.advocate.com/politics/2016/9/29/california-adopts-groundbreaking-all-gender-restroom-access-law.

Rocco, P. "Laboratories of what? American federalism and the politics of democratic subversion." In *Democratic resilience: Can the US withstand rising polarization?* edited by R. Lieberman, S. Mettler, and K. Roberts, 297–319. New York: Cambridge University Press, 2021.

Rosenberg, A. *Turning the tables: Requiring access to diaper changing stations*. Madison: Wisconsin Policy Project, 2019.

Schmitt, M. L., K. Booth, and M. Sommer. "A policy for addressing menstrual equity in schools: A case study from New York City, U.S.A." *Frontiers in Reproductive Health* 3 (2022): 1–10.

Sebert Kuhlmann, A., E. Peters Bergquist, D. Danjoint, and L. L. Wall. "Unmet menstrual hygiene needs among low-income women." *Obstetrics & Gynecology* 133, no. 2 (2019): 238–244. https://journals.lww.com/greenjournal/fulltext/2019/02000/unmet_menstrual_hygiene_needs_among_low_income.2.aspx.

Serlin, D. "Pissing without pity: Disability, gender, and the public toilet." In *Toilet: Public restrooms and the politics of sharing*, edited by H. Molotch and L. Noren, 167–185. New York: New York University Press, 2010.

Sharrow, E. A. "Sports, transgender rights and the bodily politics of cisgender supremacy." *Laws* 10, no. 3 (2021): 1–29.

Shor, B. "Individual state legislator Shor-McCarty ideology data, July 2020 update." V1 Harvard Dataverse, 2020, https://doi.org/10.7910/DVN/GZJOT3.

Shor, B., and N. McCarty. "The ideological mapping of American legislatures." *American Political Science Review* 105, no. 3 (2011): 530–551.

Silver, H., and S. M. Miller. "Social exclusion: The European approach to social disadvantage." *Indicators* 2, no. 2 (2003): 5–21.

Simon, B. "The trouble with bathrooms." *Modern American History* 4, no. 2 (2021): 201–207.

Smith, B. "Senate Democrats walk out on vote overturning 'bathroom' ordinance." *The Carolina Journal*, March 24, 2016. www.carolinajournal.com/senate-democrats-walk-out-of-vote-overturning-bathroom-ordinance/.

Solomon, D. "NH House Democrats pass bills restricting use of plastic bags, straws." *New Hampshire Union Leader (Manchester, NH)*, March 19, 2019. https://infoweb.newsbank.com/apps/news/document-view? p=WORLDNEWS&docref=news/1731CFF78A5C9A68. NewsBank.

"Squat for change: Photo of dad and baby on floor sparks call for diaper-changing stations in men's restrooms." *ABC13*, October 3, 2018. https:// abc13.com/diaper-changing-tables-in-mens-restrooms-squat-for-change/ 4399279/.

The Sustainable Development Goals report. United Nations, 2023, https:// unstats.un.org/sdgs/report/2023/The-Sustainable-Development-Goals-Report-2023.pdf.

Teizazu, H., M. Sommer, C. Gruer, et al. "'Do we not bleed?' Sanitation, menstrual management, and homelessness in the time of covid." *Columbia Journal of Gender and Law* 41 (2021): 208–217.

The General Court of the Commonwealth of Massachusetts. "An act relative to transgender anti-discrimination." 2016, https://malegislature.gov/Bills/ 189/S735.

Tischauser, L. V. *Jim Crow laws.* Santa Barbara: Greenwood, 2012.

Tisdale, E. S., and C. H. Atkins. "The sanitary privy and its relation to public health." *American Journal of Public Health and the Nation's Health* 33, no. 11 (1943): 1319–1322.

Tresca, A. J. "How the Restroom Access Act helps those with IBD." *Very Well Health*, May 2, 2020. https://web.archive.org/web/20230909205611/ https://www.verywellhealth.com/the-restroom-access-act-1942432.

Tumin, R. "Scotland makes period products free." *The New York Times*, August 15, 2022. www.nytimes.com/2022/08/15/world/europe/scotland-free-period-products.html.

"U.S. Department of Labor – restrooms and sanitation requirements." 2023, accessed November 21, 2023, www.osha.gov/restrooms-sanitation.

Van Houweling, E., and R. Botta. *Access to water and toilet facilities for the unhoused in Denver*, 2023, https://housekeysactionnetwork.com/wp-con tent/uploads/2023/09/WASH-Final-20230927.pdf.

Virginia Department of Education. "Model policies on ensuring privacy, dignity, and respect for all students and parents in Virginia's public schools." 2023, accessed January 3, 2024, www.doe.virginia.gov/programs-services/student-services/student-assistance-programming/gender-diversity.

Vishniac, M. "The new correctional afterthought: Menstruation and incarceration in the U.S.A." PhD Thesis, University of Edinburgh, 2024. https://era.ed.ac.uk/.

"The prison flow project." 2023, accessed November 27, 2023, https://theprisonflowproject.com/state-laws-around-access/.

Vleminckx, K., and J. Berghman. "Social exclusion and the welfare state: An overview of conceptual issues and policy implications." In *Social exclusion and European policy*, edited by D. Mayes, J. Berghman, and R. Salais, 27–46. Northampton: Elgar, 2001.

Weinmeyer, R. M. "Lavatories of democracy: Recognizing a right to public toilets through international human rights and state constitutional law." *University of Pennsylvania Journal of Constitutional Law* 26, no. 2 (2024): 402–470.

Weintraub, K. "Massachusetts law on transgender protections draws strong support ahead of vote." *Washington Post*, October 30, 2018, www.washingtonpost.com/national/massachusetts-law-on-transgender-protections-draws-strong-support-ahead-of-vote/2018/10/30/7c116c4c-dbe4-11e8-85df-7a6b4d25cfbb_story.html.

Weiss-Wolf, J. *Periods gone public: Taking a stand for menstrual equity.* New York: Arcade, 2017.

"U.S. Policymaking to address menstruation: Advancing an equity agenda." In *The Palgrave handbook of critical menstruation studies*, edited by C. Bobel, I. T. Winkler, B. Fahs, et al., 539–549. Singapore: Palgrave MacMillan, 2020.

Wiegand, W. A., and S. A. Wiegand. *The desegregation of public libraries in the Jim Crow south: Civil rights and local activism.* Baton Rouge: Louisiana State University Press, 2018.

Wilson, S. "State-level activism in the disability context: Ensuring protections for people with disabilities through American federalism and the Fourteenth Amendment equal protection clause." *Journal of Health & Biomedical Law* 15, no. 2 (2019): 173–204.

Wiseman, P. "Lifting the lid: Disabled toilets as sites of belonging and embodied citizenship." *The Sociological Review* 67, no. 4 (2019): 788–806.

Wolfenbarger, D. *New Deal resources on Colorado's eastern plains.* NPS Form 10-900-b: National Register of Historic Places Multiple Property Documentation Form: United States Department of the Interior – National

Parks Service, 2005. www.historycolorado.org/sites/default/files/media/document/2017/649.pdf.

World Health Organization. "Gender and Health." 2024, accessed March 19, 2024, www.who.int/health-topics/gender.

Yellin, E. *Our mothers' war: American women at home and at the front during World War II*. New York: Free Press, 2004.

Yuko, E. "Where did all the public bathrooms go?" *Bloomberg*, November 5, 2021. www.bloomberg.com/news/features/2021-11-05/why-american-cities-lost-their-public-bathrooms.

Acknowledgements

This project grew out of a first-year seminar that I teach at the University of Denver, and I am very grateful to all the students who have taken this class and helped to deepen my thinking on the topic of bathrooms and politics. Many thanks also to Tiffany Barnes and Diana O'Brien for encouraging me to write this manuscript and working with me to submit it to Cambridge Elements. For their incredibly helpful feedback, I am grateful to Jesse Acevedo, Christine Bird, Kayla Caelo, Phil Chen, Belinda Creel Davis, Christian Hosam, Monica Lemke, Robert Lieberman, Seth Masket, Abby Matthews, Lia Merivaki, Annelise Russel, Jessica Trounstine, Aloka Wanigasuriya, Kirsten Widner, Josh Wilson, and Alena Wolflink – with additional thanks to Michael Greenberger for both thoughtful comments and advice on putting together maps in R. I also thank my husband, Tim Gordon, for both his support during the time I wrote this manuscript, as well as his advice on architectural information. Finally, I gratefully acknowledge financial support from the Center on American Politics at the University of Denver and conference support from Women in Legislative Studies.

Cambridge Elements ☰

Gender and Politics

Tiffany D. Barnes

University of Texas at Austin

Tiffany D. Barnes is Professor of Political Science at the University of Texas at Austin. She is the author of *Women, Politics, and Power: A Global Perspective* (Rowman & Littlefield, 2007) and, award-winning, *Gendering Legislative Behavior* (Cambridge University Press, 2016). Her research has been funded by the National Science Foundation (NSF) and recognized with numerous awards. Barnes is the former president of the Midwest Women's Caucus and founder and director of the Empirical Study of Gender (EGEN) network.

Diana Z. O'Brien

Washington University in St. Louis

Diana Z. O'Brien is the Bela Kornitzer Distinguished Professor of Political Science at Washington University in St. Louis. She specializes in the causes and consequences of women's political representation. Her award-winning research has been supported by the NSF and published in leading political science journals. O'Brien has also served as a Fulbright Visiting Professor, an associate editor at *Politics & Gender*, the president of the Midwest Women's Caucus, and a founding member of the EGEN network.

About the Series

From campaigns and elections to policymaking and political conflict, gender pervades every facet of politics. Elements in Gender and Politics features carefully theorized, empirically rigorous scholarship on gender and politics. The Elements both offer new perspectives on foundational questions in the field and identify and address emerging research areas.

Cambridge Elements ⸗

Gender and Politics

Printed in the United States
by Baker & Taylor Publisher Services